Praise for Dermot Cole's FRANK BARR

"*News-Miner* reporter Dermot Cole offers good reading with his . . . biography of bush pilot Frank Barr. Barr . . . emerges clearly in this adventure-filled book as a fun-loving, witty, inventive man whose exploits never bore a reader. . . . Cole's text glitters with bits of Alaskana."

—Fairbanks Daily News-Miner

"Throughout the book, Cole relates harrowing stories and humorous anedotes, many of them common companions of Alaska's bush pilots: forced landings, makeshift repairs, plenty of improvising, and even weeks of stranded isolation in arctic winters. . . . *Frank Barr* is an entertaining tale of the exploits of one of Alaska's diminishing population of bush pilots. . . . A refreshing look at the not-so-distant past. . . ."

— Tundra Times

"This book is a terrific salute to a daring breed of aviator who flew the Alaska-Yukon territory in the '30s and '40s."

—Coast Book Review

"A fascinating new book from Alaska Northwest."

—Contra Costa (Walnut Creek, CA) Times

"*Frank Barr* presents a fascinating—perhaps even archetypal—life. Barr's adventuresome spirit and love of fun come through clearly in Cole's 1986 text."

—Fairbanks Daily News-Miner

Frank Barr, 1938.

FRANK BARR

Bush Pilot in Alaska and the Yukon

DERMOT COLE

ALASKA NORTHWEST BOOKS™

For Debbie

Library of Congress Cataloging-in-Publication Data

Cole, Dermot, 1953–
Frank Barr, bush pilot in Alaska and the Yukon.
Bibliography: p. 113.
1. Barr, Frank, 1903–1983. 2. Bush pilots — Alaska — Biography.
I. Title.
TL540.B357C65   1986   629.13'092'4   [B]   86-3633
ISBN 0-88240-314-1 (1986 edition)
ISBN 0-88240-525-X (Caribou Classics edition)

Caribou Classics Editor: Ellen Harkins Wheat
Cover design by Constance Bollen
Interior design and maps by Robert Chrestensen
Photographs: All photographs are from the Barr family collection unless noted otherwise.

Printed on recycled paper in the United States of America

Published by Alaska Northwest Books™
An imprint of Graphic Arts Center Publishing Company
P.O. Box 10306 • Portland, Oregon 97296-0306
503/226-2402
www.gacpc.com

Contents

Foreword

WE REMEMBER Frank Barr as another of that wonderful breed of men who were the real bush pilots of the Alaska-Yukon, the pilots who used "smooth enough" ridgetops and "pretty short and a bit soft" river bars for airports—who flew down where you could see, and who kept bearings with the same tripod trail markers and distant peaks as did the dog team drivers.

We remember a time when Barr brought in his big Pilgrim freighter from a Taku river bar with something like window boxes for skis—open-on-one-end things into which he rolled his wheels and shoved ahead of him with full power until he was safely in the air. We remember his landing and taking off from the tailing pile at Juneau because there were no facilities for his wheel plane at the Juneau airport.

We remember Eskimos reporting regularly each week at Bethel that "Barr get in," and hearing him shush-shushing up the road-house stairs to a room we often shared at the end of his mail run there—and his sealskin parka, his sealskin overnight valise—and a time we stomped the ice together at Minchumina, flapping our arms against our sides while we waited for the oil for his plane to boil on the firepot. It was something like forty-plus below and nostril drawing cold. Mount McKinley in the southeast distance stood stark against the frozen pale blue sky.

It was a perfect setting for Frank to tell me the "Kee Bird" tale—about the Far North little birds that lined up each morning along the edge of the ice floes and together flapped their wings mightily against their sides, much as we were doing while the oil would come to a boil.

That's when we learned that the "Kee Birds" were thus called because inevitably one of them would cry out, "Kee-ee-ee-RIMINEY, it's cold!"

Barr enjoyed his flying, and we know you'll enjoy these stories of his early flying days.

Robert G. Henning

—Publisher
Alaska Northwest Publishing Company
(1986)

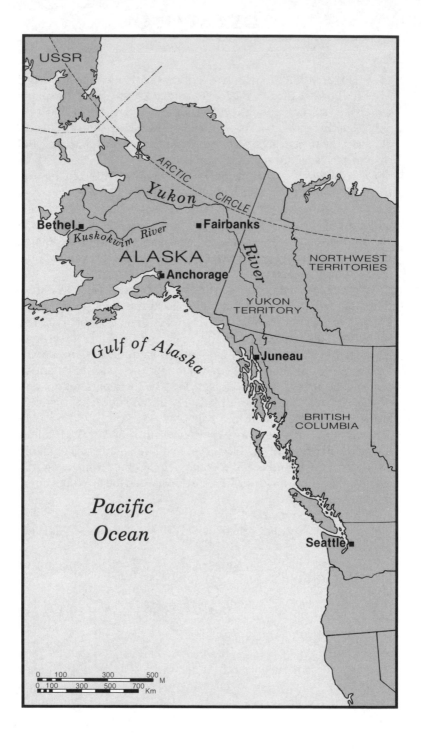

Preface

DURING THE twenty-five years he flew bush planes in Alaska, Frank Barr endured more forced landings than he could remember. Like the other Alaskan bush pilots of the 1930s and 1940s, he flew under some of the toughest conditions in the world, in aircraft usually long past their prime.

Barr was once stranded in the wilderness for six weeks, but he rebuilt his wrecked biplane and flew it home. On another occasion he was missing for five days, until a massive air search tracked him down. He was found calmly tending his signal fire. A rescue plane dropped him a supply of grub, and he walked out to safety. Later he returned to repair the damaged plane, and flew it back to Fairbanks.

Barr never lost his sense of humor, and his easy-going disposition helped him through many a close call. The slogan for his one-man, one-plane airline, Barr Air Transport, was: "If you feel you must get there in the worst way, fly with Barr."

He flew hundreds of thousands of miles, and carried thousands of passengers who wanted to cross the Alaskan wilderness "in the worst way." Though he never became rich or famous at his chosen occupation (Barr liked the old pilot's saying that "flying is better than working"), his big Pilgrim monoplane was a common sight in Juneau, Atlin, Whitehorse, Fairbanks, Bethel, and most places in-between. To many people in the Alaskan bush forty years ago, Frank Barr was their only contact with the outside world.

The roving bush pilot, who started his career with the U.S. Cavalry after World War I, chasing bandits on the Mexican border, was a natural story-teller. Barr's other exploits included a stint as a professional parachute jumper and a test pilot in the 1920s in Detroit (where he made extra money flying bootleg Canadian whiskey into the United States during Prohibition).

Archie Satterfield, a prominent Northwest author who has written extensively about aviation and Alaska, started the task of telling Frank Barr's life story. He turned the project over to me in 1982, when the press of other business made it impossible for him to continue.

I visited Barr in December of that year and stayed with him at his house in Grants Pass, Oregon, continuing the interviews which by then covered more than 1,000 typed pages. We sat around Barr's kitchen table, looking over Barr's extensive collection of old photographs as he told stories of his past. I spent two years on the book, working on it at nights and weekends when I could get time away from my job as an editor and reporter for the *Fairbanks Daily News-Miner,* where I have worked since 1976.

My primary sources were the taped interviews with Barr. I also did extensive research in back issues of Alaska newspapers in Juneau and Fairbanks. This was supplemented by regional magazines, aviation periodicals and books, as well as interviews with some of Barr's friends and contemporaries.

More than 16 years have passed since Frank Barr's death, but the tales of his time in Alaska remain important for those who want to know what aviation was like in the early days. As Barr put it, he was part of the "larger middle class" of pioneer bush pilots, who were in it not for the money or the fame, but for the flying.

—Dermot Cole
Fairbanks
(1999)

Acknowledgments

I WOULD LIKE to thank: my brother, Terrence Cole, historian at Alaska Northwest Publishing Company, and his wife, writer Marjorie K. Cole, for their editorial assistance and suggestions; Archie Satterfield for his generosity. I would also like to thank Winnie Acheson, Lyman Sands, Renee Blahuta, Claus-M. Naske, Alaska Linck, Charles Bennett and Kent Sturgis.

To Alaska Northwest Publisher Robert A. Henning is due much credit and many thanks, for helping to see that the story of his old friend Frank Barr was published.

Finally, I would like to thank my wife, Debbie Carter, for her work as an editor and her constant encouragement.

CHAPTER 1

Lost on Wolf Lake

FRANK BARR pushed back the frosted edge of his sleeping bag and listened in the darkness of the dirt-floored cabin. Awakened by the roar of the wind, Barr's first thoughts were of the Moth biplane he had tied up the night before on the frozen shore of Wolf Lake. It was November 21, 1933, and Barr was on one of his early winter trips into the wilderness of Yukon Territory.

The plane was a World War I trainer made of wire, wood, fabric and a little steel. Even in 1933, when Boeing introduced an all-metal airliner that could cross the United States in nineteen hours, Barr's biplane was an open-cockpit throwback to aviation's past. He called it *La Cucuracha,* after a popular Mexican dance-hall song about a cockroach who hates work. He had the name painted on the engine cowling in capital letters.

La Cucuracha was on skis and Barr had folded back the wings and tied the plane to some rocks along the shoreline before going to sleep. He had done all he could to protect the flimsy craft, but the screaming wind told him it might not be enough. He jumped up to take a look. He could see nothing outside except blowing snow and the tops of spruce trees that were leaning over as if pressed by a giant hand. The wind seemed to be blowing ninety miles per hour. He could do nothing except wait until morning to see whether his ticket back to civilization would survive the night.

The previous day he had flown in from Atlin, a little gold-mining town at the northern tip of British Columbia. Barr was flying cans of fuel and food to Sayea Creek, a tributary of the Liard River, so

The World War I trainer that he flew for trader Bill Strong, Barr named "La Cucuracha," after the Mexican song about the cockroach who hates work. The man standing by the plane is Charles Berry, a young mining engineer.

he could bring in a prospecting expedition the next spring. Just before sunset he had stopped at Wolf Lake, near the cabin built years earlier by an old French Canadian trapper, Napoleon Moreau.

If the storm damaged the plane, Barr knew he was entirely on his own. No one knew where he was and there was no radio nor telephone communication to the remote lake. The Alaska Highway would one day pass within fifty miles of the lake, but it wouldn't be built for another decade. There would be no search by other pilots, either, because the nearest plane was two hundred miles away over the coastal range in Juneau.

By this time aviation had gained a solid foothold in Alaska through the pioneering work of Carl Ben Eielson, Noel Wien and Joe Crosson, but progress came more slowly across the border. In the winter of 1933-34 there were practically no planes flying in the Canadian northwest above the transcontinental railroad, hundreds of miles to the south at Prince George.

As he listened to the wind, the twenty-nine-year-old pilot wasted little time worrying over what might happen and went back to sleep. He was a calm, confident man who knew something about getting out of a tight spot, having been put to the test many times before as a cavalryman, parachute jumper, test pilot and mechanic.

A short, stocky figure with a neat mustache, dark hair and brown eyes, Barr had come north eighteen months earlier with a thirty-five-man gold-hunting expedition from Detroit. When the expedition fell apart, Barr got a job flying the Moth for Bill Strong, an Englishman who ran a trading post and hauled freight on the Taku River east of Juneau.

Inadequate as it was — it could carry one passenger or about two hundred pounds of freight — the small craft could still cover as much ground in one day as a prospector did in an entire season on foot. The Moth's wings could easily be permanently clipped, however, by this severe storm.

When Barr awoke at dawn, he made a fire in the rusted Yukon stove with kindling saved from the night before. Moss chinking between the logs had fallen out in several places and the cabin was drafty and cold. He had to stand very close to the stove to feel any heat, and even then he could see his breath. Opening the cabin door, he found a silent white landscape. The wind had ceased and the temperature had tumbled to fifty below zero. While preparing oatmeal mush for breakfast, Barr heard a knock on the door. He invited the visitor in for a cup of coffee.

"Cold today," Barr said.

During the storm on Wolf Lake, Barr's flimsy Moth biplane flipped over on its back. Barr said the old World War I trainer looked like a dead duck with its feet in the air.

Barr and two Indians took the wings off the wrecked Moth (on left) and rolled the fuselage right side up. The temperature dropped as low as fifty below zero, and it took Barr six weeks to get the plane back in the air.

"Uh-huh," said his guest.

Native people don't like to rush into things and neither did Barr. They drank their coffee and it was a few minutes before the Indian broke the bad news. "Airplane, she upside down," he said, flipping his outstretched hand over. The two men finished their coffee and went out to inspect the damage.

As the Indian had said, they found the plane with its skis facing stiffly skyward like a cartoon version of a dead duck. In addition, a steel strut supporting the upper wing was badly damaged. The fabric wing-covering had been ripped in several spots and the top of the rudder was smashed. Several wing ribs were crushed and worst of all, six inches had been lopped off one end of the wooden propeller.

The situation was as clear as the weather was cold: Barr could either repair the plane and fly it home, or walk about sixty miles across the mountains on snowshoes to Teslin.

Attempting such a walk without adequate provisions would have been foolhardy in that weather. Three years earlier, pilot E.J. "Paddy" Burke of Atlin had died after he tried to walk out from a forced landing in this same area. Starvation, exposure and a kidney ailment killed Burke. His passenger and mechanic nearly starved before they were rescued two months later.

To avoid a repeat of the Burke disaster, Barr's only real choice was to repair the plane and fly away. It wasn't going to be easy. He was carrying only a skimpy set of tools and a small emergency kit with a wire for snaring rabbits, a .22 caliber rifle, and a few spare parts. Luckily he had a fair-sized stockpile of canned and dried food.

Because it was mild the previous day, Barr hadn't bothered to drain the oil from the plane's engine. He considered himself lucky that he was carrying extra oil because, when the plane flipped over, the oil leaked out and was now in a frozen pool mixed with snow. He saved some by carrying big black chunks back to the cabin in a bucket and heating the frozen goop on the stove to separate the oil from the water.

The young man who'd stopped by for coffee was one of a family of Indians who had their winter trapline base cabin on the lake. He and another fellow helped Barr remove the wings and flip the plane up onto its skis.

Work on the airplane went slowly because temperatures remained far below zero for weeks and occasionally dipped to minus fifty. Most of the repairs were one-man jobs that had to be done slowly in the bitter cold. To start a nut or hold a small screw he could take his mittens off, but only for a few seconds at a time. Any longer than that and his fingers would freeze to the metal.

Gathering food, water and firewood proved to be nearly as time-consuming as work on the mangled plane. Barr had never used snares before, but the Indians told him where to set them and he put out five near the cabin. On his first attempt he found a rabbit in each one.

He supplemented his meat supply by hunting ptarmigan that he stored with the rabbits in the natural deepfreeze on the windowsill of the cabin. The Indians gave him frozen whitefish in exchange for a little salt and sugar, and it was a welcome addition to his diet. He ate great, steaming hunks of fish topped with canned butter and blackberry jam. For drinking water, Barr had to melt buckets of the fine, powdery snow to get a few cups.

He wore two suits of heavy woolen underwear, extra-thick trousers and shirt and three pairs of heavy boot socks with half-inch-thick felt insoles in his moccasins. He was so well insulated that one day he burned a saucer-sized hole in the back of his trousers before he could feel the heat from the stove.

The cabin had no lantern, so he fashioned an Eskimo lamp with a coffee-can lid filled with spare engine oil. With a rag for a wick, the lamp gave a dim light and produced a greasy black smoke that hung inside the cabin.

About three weeks after his arrival, the Natives left to tend to their traplines and Barr was alone with *La Cucuracha*. As the weeks passed, he filled his days with work on the biplane and his daily chores.

"The loneliness didn't bother me," Barr recalled years later. "I had always been content alone and there was never a doubt that I would pull through."

He flattened an empty gas can and nailed it over the leading edge of the wing. He patched up the broken windshield by drilling a series of holes and lacing them together. This would give him some protection from the super-cold wind in the cockpit. The broken strut which held the upper wing to the fuselage was made of lightweight tubing. He had no metal to make a new one, so he straightened the broken metal and tied a hickory ax handle to it. He lashed the ax handle tightly to the strut with strips of moosehide.

Barr's biggest problem was the propeller, which had to be recut by hand. He had no tools to duplicate the precise factory cut, so he did the best he could with a hunting knife. He trimmed the jagged end of the prop with his knife, made a paper model, and tried to cut the other end to match. This was an exacting job because an unbalanced prop could shake the plane to pieces.

When he finished whittling it down, he didn't know whether the shortened prop would provide enough power to get the plane up to its takeoff speed of 38 miles per hour.

After six weeks of work, he was nearly ready to find out, but first he needed a runway. He spent a full day on snowshoes, stamping out a narrow half-mile runway in the snow ahead of the airplane. He walked over it several times to get the snow hardened, and returned to the cabin for a dinner of boiled rice and tea with sugar. He hoped the wind wouldn't come up during the night and cover his tracks.

In the morning he lightened the plane's load as much as possible, leaving all equipment behind except for his snowshoes and sleeping bag. He warmed the engine with a plumber's torch and was ready to go. The engine started with a cough and settled down to a welcome roar. He opened the throttle a bit more than halfway, enough to get the plane moving under normal circumstances, but with the shortened prop it remained frozen in its tracks. He gave it full throttle and the biplane began sliding reluctantly down his homemade runway.

The engine howled as the plane bounced down the lake and gathered speed ever so slowly. *La Cucuracha* eventually staggered into the air, but it moved like an overloaded barge in heavy seas and couldn't climb more than a few feet above the lake.

"We were so near a stall that the controls felt loose and sloppy in my hands. Luckily, Wolf Lake is five miles wide and by the time we got to the opposite shore we had gained enough altitude to clear the trees," Barr said. He wondered to himself how long the screaming engine would go on before it began scattering nuts and bolts across the countryside.

"After leaving the lake I could see only timber, rocks and deep ravines below — and not far below. There were sixty miles more to go, which meant about one hour at the rate of speed we were plowing through the air."

Barr had no trouble finding something to take his mind off the overworked engine and prop. Every time he went through rough air he glanced at the ax handle and moosehide holding the wing strut in place. A sudden, unexpected downdraft could break the splint and the wings would fold around him.

"I definitely did not feel at ease. I strained my ears for the slightest change in the sound of the engine, checked possible landing spots, and tried to hold the plane up with my stomach muscles. And I was cold! An open cockpit plane in the sub-Arctic was not my idea of solid comfort."

He covered his face to keep the wind from freezing his skin and peered through his goggles, holding a steady course to the southwest for Teslin. The rough terrain eventually gave way to the smooth surface of Nisutlin Bay, but he wasn't ready to celebrate yet.

With the engine running at full throttle, the plane was consuming an enormous amount of gas. The fuel gauge was nearing the empty mark when Barr saw Teslin in the distance. He sat tensely in his seat, watching for a smooth enough spot among the snowdrifts for a forced landing, and glancing back at the flickering fuel needle.

Somehow *La Cucuracha* managed to squeeze just enough distance out of its gas supply, and Barr glided to a perfect landing on the ice in front of the Teslin trading post. There was less than a cup of gas left in the tank when he shut the engine off. He climbed stiffly out of the plane and flailed his arms about to get his blood flowing again.

Bill Irvine, the Royal Canadian Mounted Policeman stationed in the little village, came down to meet the lost pilot. Barr went to Irvine's quarters and enjoyed a hot bath, scrubbing the residue of his motor oil lamp off his skin. He topped that off with a meal of moose steak and apple pie at the home of Robin and Sue McCleary, who ran the trading post.

The next day he checked his plane for signs of undue wear from the rough Wolf Lake flight. Nothing seemed to be dangerously loose or worn. He tightened the ax handle splint, filled the tank with gas, and was back in Atlin in another hour.

In the years to come, the story of what happened during those six cold weeks on Wolf Lake became known to pilots throughout the North. It helped earn Barr a reputation as one of the most resourceful of the pioneer Arctic bush pilots.

CHAPTER 2

Those Who Didn't

IN THE BARR FAMILY there were always two classes of people: Those who stayed home and became solid citizens and those who didn't. "My father was a didn't and I was a didn't," Frank said.

The younger Barr started life as Lucien Francis Barr on August 22, 1903, on his grandfather's Illinois farm. He was proud that he was born in the same year that the Wright "boys" first flew, but he never cared for his given name. Lucien was not a name of which he was proud. Frank was much more his style, or just Barr, as most of his friends always knew him.

Frank's father, Willard, was a drifter who tried on careers as casually as if they were overcoats. In 1887 at 22, he quit his job as a pharmacist and began to travel. He toured the West and ended up on an illegal sealing schooner in the Bering Sea. He was a clerk at the World's Fair in Chicago and an investor in sheep in South Dakota. A steep drop in wool prices and the advent of the Spanish-American War led him out of the sheep business and into Cuba, where he was promoted to corporal and served as a war correspondent. After the war, he returned to Illinois, married Grace Crump, and tried to become a solid citizen.

She had grown up in Lott, Texas, and was visiting relatives near Bridgeport, Illinois, when she met Willard. Her family had sent her there because they wanted her to forget all about the son of a drunken printer she was going out with, back in Texas.

When Grace met Willard and fell in love with him, he was running a 4,600-tree apple orchard. Before long they were married and living on the Barr farm in Lawrence County. Willard and Grace had four sons — Eugene, Lucien Francis, Willard Jr. and Paul.

They lived on the second floor of the two-story farm house, while Willard's parents — Jacob and Katherine — lived downstairs. The close living quarters did not make for domestic tranquility. Willard's mother tried to run the show, but Grace was not accustomed to being bossed around and they didn't get along.

Frank's mother had made at least one Christmas trip back to Texas to visit her parents before she began a second in 1906. She took the youngest child, Paul, and left the rest of the children at the family farm. While in Texas, she received a telegram that her husband was missing.

Willard had driven a horse and buggy to town that January day in 1907, and left a pair of shoes at the Eagle Shoe Store. His horse showed up at home that night alone. It was several days before his body was found in the Wabash River.

Some people thought he was despondent over his wife's absence and had committed suicide, but others said that was nonsense. They guessed he had stopped for a drink of water to take with his heart medicine, had a heart attack, and fell into the river. Either way, there was always a mystery over his death and the Barr family blamed it on Grace — unfairly in Frank's view. Her relatives in Texas said she fully intended to return to her husband and sons until Willard died. After his death, however, she stayed in Texas and never came back to Illinois, perhaps expecting that her relations with Willard's mother would only get worse.

Frank's youngest brother, Paul, stayed with Grace, and Willard Jr. later ran away from home and was sent to Texas as well. It would be another fifty years before Frank saw his mother or two younger brothers again.

Frank and his older brother, Eugene, remained in Illinois and were adopted by their father's brother Walter. Walter was a doctor and writer who called himself G. Walter Barr or Granville Barr, whichever sounded more important at the time. A small, reserved man who wore a large, flowing beard and round glasses, he practiced medicine from 1884 until 1898. At thirty-eight he gave up medicine to follow a life-long urge to write for a living. Over the years he worked as a novelist, newspaperman and public relations man in several states. While employed by the *Yorkville Enquirer* in South Carolina, he wrote 25,000 to 30,000 words a week, turning out twice as much copy as the average newsman, his obituary said.

When Frank went north to the Yukon, he was surprised to find a copy of his uncle's turn-of-the-century novel, *Shacklett, Evolution of a Statesman*, on a dusty bookshelf in a remote roadhouse. In it the hero has this advice for would-be statesmen: "Read up on the life of Lincoln. It's the bible of the really successful politician who aspires above the legislature."

Walter's novel never gained a big following, and he moved around frequently with his adopted children. They lived in Keokuk, Iowa, two or three times. He was city editor of the *Daily Gate* newspaper in Keokuk, and he did publicity work on the Keokuk Dam, spreading the word that the dam, which stretched nearly a mile across the Mississippi, contained as much rock as one of the great pyramids of Egypt.

Keokuk, located on a limestone bluff high above the spot where the Des Moines River empties into the Mississippi, was a manufacturing center for the pioneer Middle West from the 1840s on. In the days before the railroad it was known as the Gate City, not only for Iowa but to the north and west as well, because of its position at the foot of the Des Moines rapids. Steamboats were unable to go beyond this point and their cargo had to be shipped overland, or transferred to other boats upstream.

The city streets were made of brick and lined with towering elms and maples that shut out the sun in the summer. Many of the gabled white houses had stained-glass windows and predated the Civil War. The view from the edge of the river bluff was said to be the best the Mississippi could offer between St. Paul and Memphis.

Keokuk is just upstream from Hannibal, Missouri, and Samuel Clemens — Mark Twain — once worked in Keokuk in a print shop owned by Clemens' brother. Barr loved the adventure of life on the river and, like Huckleberry Finn, he had an independent streak as wide as the Mississippi.

On one occasion Barr announced plans to take off from school during the winter and go camping south of town on the river. His uncle said no, but Frank went anyway. For three or four days he and another boy camped in Glen Ellen, a beautiful wild spot with high cliffs and tall trees.

His uncle officially disapproved, but he admired the boy's spirit of adventure. Years later he wrote to Frank, "In your camping out you never were Boy Scoutish, but more of the old prospector type."

Those camping trips did not help Frank's grades in school, however. As his uncle put it, "You were always near the top, and actually there in learning as distinguished from grades."

Frank learned early to fend for himself. He worked in an ice cream parlor during high school, and ate in restaurants most of the time. When World War I ended, Barr's brother, Eugene, returned after serving on the Destroyer *Wilkes.* Although Eugene was only sixteen, he was a man of the world in the eyes of fifteen-year-old Frank. On Eugene's suggestion, the two ran away.

Barr had run away before, but this time he was gone for good. He had completed only two years of high school when he took to the road. He and Eugene hitchhiked to Indianapolis, getting rides on hay wagons and in cars. As soon as they arrived in the city, they both got jobs in a restaurant so they could eat.

"It was a fifth-class restaurant, with bare boards and bare tables, and they had a steam table to serve from," Frank said. Frank did dishes, while Eugene served up steaming hot food to customers. One night as he walked the city streets after work, Frank stopped in a small, quiet family saloon with sawdust on the floor. Hanging on the wall was a lithograph of a jockey leading a horse, and Barr never forgot it.

The jockey was exercising the horse, and coming along behind was a fellow pushing a shovel. Underneath it was a caption: "The only way you can make money following the ponies." At the time, Barr had no money to gamble even if he had been so inclined. His shoes had holes in them and he couldn't afford new ones, but the Barr brothers had no intention of returning home to their uncle.

One day Eugene ran into the hotel room with a pair of used shoes for his brother. Frank threw away his old ones and was walking tall for a couple of days, until the owner of the shoes, another resident of the flea-bag hotel, demanded them back. Frank was shoeless until his brother could scrape up another pair.

The two Barr brothers took a step up from poverty when they landed jobs with the Atkins Saw Company. Frank was to reach into a furnace with a long rod and pull out white-hot saw blades. He'd dunk the blades into a hot oil bath and set them aside to cool off. They put Frank on piece work because he was fast, and the extra money began to burn a hole in his pocket. One of his friends at the saw company, a young man named Frenzel, suggested they go to Chicago to see the town. Frank split up with his brother and went off with Frenzel.

The Windy City was living up to its reputation during the winter of 1919, when Barr and his friend took the grand tour. They weathered it in style at the Morrison Hotel until the money ran out. Then it was back to State Street for the two penniless, shivering, tourists, Barr dressed in a light topcoat and Frenzel in a leather jacket.

"It was cold," Barr said. "We were willing to go anywhere it wasn't cold. Here were these recruiting posters. So we flipped coins to decide whether we would join the Coast Guard or the Army or the Navy."

The Army won. They walked into the recruiting office and the sergeant at the desk took a long look at the two young teenagers. He asked, "How old are you? Eighteen?" The two nodded their heads and the sergeant asked what they had in mind. Barr said they wanted to go "someplace where it's warm."

"Well, how about the Cavalry in Texas, down on the Mexican border?" the sergeant asked. That sounded good because Barr liked horses, having ridden them on his grandfather's farm. He could already feel the warm Texas sun as he signed the enlistment papers.

He didn't want his uncle to track him down and force him to return home, so he gave an alias. He remembered seeing a plumbing truck in Keokuk with the name "Roy M. King" on the side, and he liked the sound of it. He signed himself Roy M. King.

Before long, "King" and Frenzel were riding a train to Texas. The short, cocky kid was well on his way to joining his father as one of those who didn't.

Barr said the hours he spent on stable duty in the Cavalry, cleaning up manure, helped him become a good aviator in later years, because he had learned to "pile it here and pile it there and then pile it on an escort wagon and haul it away." In 1923 he transferred from the Cavalry to the Army Air Service, and was sent to radio school at Chanute Field, Illinois, where there were no stables to clean.

14

CHAPTER 3

A Cavalryman on the Mexican Border

THE FEBRUARY chill in Marfa, Texas, didn't match the picture of paradise painted by the recruiter back in Chicago. Barr, who was now known as Private Roy King by everyone except Frenzel, was assigned to the Fifth Cavalry in the wild Big Bend country.

"I wondered if it would ever warm up down there," he said. "Our hands would crack open from the cold, and that winter, 1919, was the time of the big flu."

Barr was in the hospital two or three weeks with the flu. Others weren't so lucky. "Every morning they'd cart another body or two out," he said, "but I managed to survive."

The Fifth Cavalry had recently been transferred to Marfa from Fort Bliss, near El Paso, and the troopers lived in tents while the cement barracks with wooden roofs were being built. Marfa is in wide open, flat, treeless country with large cattle ranches hidden in the mountains to the north and south. The altitude is about two thousand feet. It was sandy. When they ate they had to dump the sand out of their plates, and at night they'd have to shake sand out of their sheets before going to bed.

The troops were there to keep the peace on a frontier that had been troubled since Mexican bandits began making cattle raids into Texas in the 1850s. From 1912 to 1920 there was intense border conflict, spurred by Mexican revolutions, Pancho Villa, prohibition enforcement and World War I. Villa's heyday was over by the time Barr arrived, but on several occasions his unit was called out to chase raiders from south of the border. Somehow the outlaws always managed to escape before the cavalry could catch them.

Barr was in M Troop, which spent most of the time on routine training and drill work. He cleaned stables, worked in the kitchen and patrolled the camp on guard duty. The cavalrymen also had daily training on horseback. The soldiers rode twenty to forty miles a day on patrols, and slept in the dust when it was hot and in the mud when it rained.

The horses got excellent care because they were the only means of transportation in that wild, rugged country. "After a long, hard day's march you took care of the horse, watered him, groomed him and fed him before you ever looked out for yourself," Barr said. Some were heavy, slow animals, while others were sleek and fast. They were kept in a big corral with a seven-foot fence around it.

"On stable duty you'd go down there and there'd be from 100 to 120 horses staying overnight, and you'd look at that and wonder if there was a conspiracy against you, because you had to rake all of that up and put it in piles," he said. This training, Barr claimed, helped him become a good aviator in later years because he had to "pile-it here and pile-it there and then pile-it on an escort wagon and haul it away."

To groom the horses, the men would have to line them up and comb them by command. "They'd be on the picket line with dust all over them and you could look down and see dust rising like a storm. The dust and dandruff would get in our eyes and sting," he said. The sergeant in charge would shout: "Groom head, neck and shoulders." Then later, "back and belly." And then "tail and dock."

The officers insisted that the dock — the part of a horse's anatomy just under the tail — be as well cared for as the rest of the horse.

The big Missouri mules were harder to handle than the horses. "The trouble was, they knew as much as the men did," Barr said. The soldiers had to put blinders on the mules just to get packs onto them. When Barr was transferred to the signal section, they used mules to carry the old spark gap code transmitters. One mule carried the two chests for the radio outfit, while a second mule carried the generator. The generator had a big hand crank on each side and it was very difficult to turn. The men struggling to wind the generator in the hot Texas sun always thought the operator, tapping out a message on the key, was going too slowly.

Barr also learned semaphore signalling with flags and became adept with the wigwag code, which was the same as the radio code. Where he really excelled, however, was on the rifle range. The soldiers spent many hours practicing with Springfield Model 19-3 rifles and Model 19-11 Colt automatic pistols. Even in 1920, those

"Roy M. King," alias for Frank Barr, riding with the members of the 3rd Platoon, 5th U.S. Cavalry, Camp Travis, Texas, 1922. "King," the name under which Barr enlisted because he was underage, is in the back row, sixth man from the right.

---

were the cavalryman's main weapons along with the saber.

Barr, who had shot rabbits with a .22 back in Illinois, and had excellent eyesight, soon won an expert rating on the rifle range. He was the best shot in the outfit, and in 1922 he won third place in the marksmanship contest at Fort Travis. By then he was teaching marksmanship. He became so comfortable with the .45 automatic that he carried one in Alaska, instead of switching to a higher-powered weapon. "I was so familiar with it I could use it even if a brown bear got me down on the ground. I wouldn't have to open up a book and read how to use the thing."

For pistol practice, the men would line up shoulder-to-shoulder on horseback and charge toward silhouette targets. The targets would be turned to face the horsemen for a few seconds as they galloped ahead. The men had a choice of firing straight ahead or to the rear after they passed the target. One soldier from Pennsylvania always forgot that he wasn't supposed to shoot sideways at the target as he rode by, because he might hit a fellow soldier. Once he began shooting, he invariably kept on until his ammo was gone. "He never killed anybody, but there was no reason why he didn't," Barr said.

Barr, alias Roy M. King, did well in the cavalry. He entered as a private making $16 a month. In three years he was earning $30

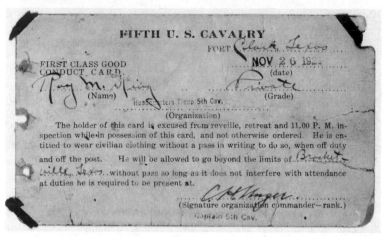

"Roy M. King's" good conduct card.

---

a month and had been promoted to sergeant, largely because of his ability as a rifle instructor.

The men he rode and trained with were an odd mix of career soldiers who had seen action as far back as the Spanish-American War, and raw recruits who had never even seen a horse. Peck Haney was one of the old-timers. He had gone to college and he was an intelligent soldier, but he liked being an ordinary cavalryman more than anything else. Haney went up and down in rank like a yo-yo. He was promoted to sergeant a few times, but on each occasion he'd cross the border to celebrate, get drunk, and wind up with a demotion. Haney finally made one trip too many. He went on leave, but was never heard from again.

Another old-timer Barr respected was a supply sergeant named Matthews, who could scrounge anything if he put his mind to it. A friend of Barr's lost his pistol and he went to Matthews looking for help. The Army kept close watch on all firearms and the loss of a gun could be grounds for a stay in the guardhouse. Like a magician, Matthews saved the soldier's neck by producing a pistol the next day. On another occasion Matthews came up with a horse for a troop commander who found out he was one short.

There were also those who just didn't fit in. Frenzel, the man Barr had enlisted with, was assigned to the records office. His job gave him access to his own personnel files and he changed some dates and got himself discharged a year early. An early departure was in the cards for another soldier, a New Yorker who was crossing the country on a motorcycle when he ran out of money in Texas and enlisted.

He could never get the knack of riding a horse, which put him at a disadvantage as a cavalryman. He would put the reins down on the horse's neck, lean on the pommel of the saddle with both hands and say "Go," but the horse wouldn't listen. The men called him "Goofy," but he wasn't entirely stupid, as Barr and the others soon discovered. One day the unit was lined up on the drill field when he walked out of headquarters waving a blue discharge in his hand. It meant he was being released for "the good of the service."

"I may be Goofy, but I've got one of these," he called out. Barr ran into him again some years later at a radio school at Chanute Field, Illinois. Goofy, then dressed in an Army Air Service uniform, said he enlisted in the Air Service under an alias after getting kicked out of the cavalry.

Barr had his own experience with switching names in the service. When he re-enlisted he did so under his real name. After his three-year cavalry tour was up in 1922, he went back to being Lucien Francis Barr and switched to the Army Air Service as a hardened veteran of nineteen.

He had first seen an airplane in 1920, when one of the Jennies used for patrol work on the Mexican border had crash-landed on the Marfa drill field. He took a picture of the wreck with its nose in the ground and the tail up in the air. "I didn't know much about airplanes and didn't care much at the time. It wasn't until after some of the men were discharged and went up to join the Army Air Service at Kelly Field that I became interested."

The saddle-weary cavalrymen were thrilled by the Air Service. With not a horse in the outfit and the men riding in luxury in Army trucks, it sounded like an easy life for an old soldier. They wrote back about what wonderful food and what interesting work they had. The work didn't consist of cleaning stables, either. It was mechanical work, electrical work. A visit to Kelly Field near San Antonio convinced Barr that the Air Service was the place to be, and he enlisted. He was assigned to the Headquarters Squadron of the 3rd Attack Group and worked as a clerk-typist in the office.

Barr was doing his job and carrying a typewriter in his lap the day he got his first airplane ride.

The pilot was a Lieutenant Zettle. He led thirteen airplanes toward a clearing in the brush where a training mission was to be based. Trucks had already hauled all the equipment except the planes out to the site and Barr was carrying the typewriter he would use in the operations tent.

The planes were De Havilland DH-4 "flying coffins." Cloth-covered World War I leftovers, they were made of spruce and held together with wire and bolts. They were assigned to the border patrol, assisting the Cavalry in the war against smuggling, illegal entry and bandits.

As they neared the end of the short flight, Zettle circled overhead to wait for the other pilots to land. Barr shifted the bulky typewriter and felt the wind in his face as he watched what unfolded below. One by one the other planes descended into trouble. The pilot who had marked the landing field didn't think the gopher holes in the field would be a problem, but they were everywhere and the pilots could not avoid hitting them.

Some planes broke their landing gear as they landed; others flipped over. When the twelfth plane rolled to a stop, Zettle aimed for a spot that looked clear of gopher holes and disabled airplanes. He came in a bit too low, though, and to avoid ramming a fence he jammed the airplane into the ground and bounced over the fence. On the other side he made a perfect three-point landing without damaging the plane, the passenger or the typewriter.

Shortly after Barr went to work at Kelly Field, General Billy Mitchell, the pioneer believer in military air power, arrived for an inspection of the men and their airplanes. The troops were in drill formation, dressed in their best uniforms, ornaments and belt buckles shining in the sun, when Mitchell arrived.

Later that day the pilots put on an aerial review and the "flying coffins" lived up to their reputation as the dignitaries and troops watched. Two planes, overloaded with machine guns, stalled making tight turns at low altitude and crashed and burned. A third plane flew into a water tank beyond the far edge of the field. Total casualties: Three pilots and three gunners.

Barr stayed in the Air Service for a year and a half, but he didn't get the opportunity nor the ambition to become a pilot until he was a civilian again. In 1924, after finishing radio school and installing a high-powered radio station at Rockwell Field in San Diego, he was discharged. A written job offer for eighty cents an hour from an Iowa electrical contractor convinced the Army that he could better himself on the outside, so his release was approved. To make it official, Barr needed the signature of his commanding officer at Rockwell.

When Barr knocked on the captain's door, the officer was inside fighting to get a mattress up the stairs, and he was in a sour mood as he walked over to sign the papers ending Barr's military career. The captain lugging the mattress that day was Henry H. "Hap" Arnold, who later became the first commanding general of the U.S. Air Force.

Arnold's signature had hardly dried before Barr, now twenty-one, was headed back east on a used Harley Davidson motorcycle. He went through Winnemucca, a small Nevada town, and pulled up to an old-fashioned gas pump next to the boardwalk. As he stopped, he noticed his motorcycle was attracting quite a bit of attention in the sleepy town.

"I guess you don't get too many motorcycles through here," Barr said to the garage owner.

"Well, no, but we had two last summer," the owner answered. As he shook the dust off his clothes, Barr asked whether they had found the going as rough as he did on the bumpy roads.

"I guess so. I've got both of them out back behind the garage."

Barr persevered over the rough trails and after visiting his uncle in Iowa, stopped in Detroit, the city a friend in the Air Service had talked much about.

It was there he learned to fly.

In the mid-1920s in Detroit, Barr learned how to fly, but he also perfected the art of coming down — the hard way — by parachute. He made exhibition jumps around the Midwest, and became a jumper with the 107th Observation Squadron of the Michigan National Guard. After 75 jumps Barr quit parachute jumping because, he said, it "was one trade where you couldn't work your way up."

CHAPTER 4

Flying High in Detroit

THE LEAP FROM automobiles to airplanes was an easy one for Detroit in the Roaring '20s. Inhabitants of the Motor City dreamed of repeating in the air their success on the ground. "In an auto you can go wherever land exists," Henry Ford said. "In an airplane you can go wherever man can breathe."

Ford organized a Detroit-Chicago airline and in June of 1926 began testing the Ford Trimotor, an 11- to 15-passenger model that became the most popular plane in America. While Ford was building "the Tin Goose," the Detroit Aviation Society sponsored the polar flights of Sir George Hubert Wilkins and Carl Ben Eielson. In 1904 the city's business leaders had sponsored automobile tours to publicize highway travel. Now they organized a series of air tours designed to convince a skeptical public of the reliability of the airplane.

Shortly after Barr arrived in Detroit, the Army created the 107th Observation Squadron of the National Guard. He became a charter member and employee of the outfit, which was equipped with three Jennies, the wartime biplane that launched the barnstorming age.

Detroit's contagious enthusiasm for flight soon had Sgt. L.F. Barr in its grip and he never got over it.

Barr's job consisted of making out payrolls and helping the mechanics keep the planes airworthy. The men who flew the planes were all World War I veterans. After a little quiet lobbying, they agreed to bend the rules and teach Barr to fly.

Whenever he could, he rode as a passenger on training flights. The pilots would let him take the controls, once they got away from squadron headquarters. He learned spins and stalls and everything else they could teach him, with two notable exceptions: No one would permit Barr to take off or land. The pilots insisted on taking control during the most critical moments of flight, because they'd have to take the blame for an accident. As a result, Barr had nearly sixty hours in the air before he ever took off.

That gap in his training was filled one warm summer day when a friend pulled up to the squadron hangar in a new open-cockpit Travelair he had just purchased. The friend, Bill Matheson, asked Barr whether he wanted to take it up for a test flight.

Barr accepted and after collecting his helmet and goggles, he took off with Matheson in the front seat. He assumed there were controls in the front cockpit, as there were on virtually all trainers, and that Matheson was going along to make sure Frank didn't get into trouble. The young pilot flew uneventfully around Rouge Park for twenty minutes. It wasn't until he had landed on the grass and taxied over to the gas tanks, to give Matheson a free fill up with government gas, that Barr noticed there were no controls in the front seat. Matheson had simply gone along for the ride.

While Barr spent more and more time learning how to fly an airplane, he also studied the art of coming down the hard way. Parachutes had been put to practical use by the Germans at the end of World War I, but it wasn't until after the war that Americans began to use them as a matter of course. Although some pilots still held to the notion that parachutes wouldn't work, the military soon made them standard equipment.

Aircraft engines were unreliable in those days and a parachute improved the margin of safety, as long as the plane had enough altitude that the pilot could survive a jump. This was amply demonstrated in 1922, when an Army pilot saved his own life by bailing out of a disabled airplane in Ohio. The Army began parachute training courses at Chanute Field, Illinois, and when the 107th Observation Squadron was given a chance to send a student in 1926, Barr volunteered.

In class they learned how to fold, sew and rig parachutes, and watched as dummies with chutes attached were dropped from the lower wing of a high-flying biplane. After six weeks of theory, Barr and the other students were ready for their graduation exercise — their first jump.

Under bright, sunny skies, ten students and instructor Sgt. Tug

Wilson, one of the few parachute experts of the day, climbed into a single-engine Fokker transport. Each man checked the chute of the man ahead of him as he waited his turn to jump. Barr was the last man to go, but as he stood at the door, he saw something was wrong with the chute on the man who had just jumped. His chute had left the pack, but instead of being strung out in a straight line behind him, it appeared to be all bunched up, and it stayed that way. His body was partly obscured by the billowing silk, but "I could see his arms flailing as is he were fighting something," Barr said.

When Wilson shouted "Ready," Barr saw the parachute, now a dim spot far below, finally inflate the way it was supposed to. He had no way of knowing whether the chute had opened in time to save the man hanging beneath it.

In an instant, Wilson ordered "Go" and Barr leaped into the air. The plane roared out of sight and all was silent. Stretched out 3,000 feet beneath him were tiny squares of rich green farmland and a one-square-mile landing zone. He loved the sensation of a 120-mile-per-hour free fall.

"Facing downward, lips apart, the rush of air into my mouth puffed out my cheeks. I could hear and feel the wind tearing at my helmet and clothes. The objects on the ground getting bigger fast."

When Barr yanked the ripcord and the canopy streamed out above him, it was "as though an enormous giant had grabbed me by the collar and hauled back. My head jerked forward and my heels snapped together." He glanced up at the silken canopy glistening above, and felt he was floating in space.

Barr landed smoothly, and to his relief discovered that so had the sergeant who'd jumped just ahead of him. It turned out that the other man's chute hadn't opened properly because his head was caught in the shroud lines of his pilot chute, a small parachute designed to fly off first, pulling the main canopy away. The sergeant said he untangled his head and threw the pilot chute to the side just in time.

Returning to Detroit, Barr put his new skills to good use. He packed all the chutes for the squadron and one of them saved the commander's life when he jumped from a crippled plane.

On weekends, Barr borrowed a chute and made exhibition jumps in Detroit and towns all over the state. He worked with many a Michigan barnstormer who would rent a large grass field on the edge of a town and advertise plane rides at two or three dollars a head. As an added attraction, the parachute jump would help insure a good crowd of potential riders for the barnstormer. Barr's jump would usually be billed in a newspaper ad as a "death-defying leap from 2,000 feet."

As was the custom, Barr received no pay, but got a one-way trip with the pilot and the chance to pass the hat among the crowd. Barr had a regular routine before long. First he'd stand on the wing of the plane and describe the action of the chute and the altitude he would jump from. Then he'd have a pretty girl or two work the crowd for donations. The least they ever made was $3.50, but on a good day they might collect $50 or $75.

After the jump, Barr and his helpers would take the proceeds to a restaurant and divide the profits. Occasionally, unexpected hitches would make things exciting.

Once he barely escaped injury at a county fair in Bad Axe, Michigan. The Army's Irwin parachute was reliable, but it didn't have a great deal of maneuverability. The jumper who could guess the exact speed of the wind would come closest to hitting his target. A bad guess could be fatal.

On this day Barr knew as soon as he'd left the plane that the wind was stronger than he had expected. As he drifted down toward the crowd the gusts nearly blew him into the roof of the grandstand. The thrilled spectators thought his landing a few yards in front of them was all part of the show.

Barr never injured himself parachuting, but he was a pallbearer at the funerals of three fellow jumpers. One of them, a man named Kowalski, always yelled, "St. Peter, here I come!" before he jumped. One day at Burns Field in Detroit, Kowalski's chute fouled. Barr watched as he hit the meadow alongside the landing strip. The jumper's body flattened the wet spring grass and the back of his white coveralls was stained green. Forever after Barr thought that "the odor of crushed grass on a warm summer day is the smell of death."

After seventy-five successful jumps, Barr gave up parachute jumping because he found it "was one trade where you couldn't work your way up."

He began to concentrate on flying and worked his way up as an aviator. He concocted a plan to buy a used Pheasant biplane that was for sale in upper Michigan. Barr's friend Lynn Staples borrowed $300 from an aunt and the two of them bought the plane sight unseen. They figured any airplane was worth at least $300.

He and Staples drove up to the small farm outside of Bay City where their new possession was parked, and dug it out of the weeds.

The previous owner said the Pheasant flew well, but he warned Barr that it "hunted" a little. That meant it would be a little unstable, but the problem was not unusual in a used plane and Barr thought he could handle the old bird.

The plane had some old cotton patches on the fabric wings and some rust here and there, but overall Barr and Staples liked its looks. There was an old cushion for a seat, a safety belt and a full complement of instruments — oil pressure gauge, altimeter and air-speed gauge. Each cylinder on the OX-5 engine gave off exhaust flames of a different color — from blue to a dull smoky red — but the plane hopped off the ground quickly and Barr wondered why such a fine airplane was sold at a rock bottom price.

He found out a few moments later, when he eased back on the throttle. The nose quickly dropped and the plane began to lose altitude. He pulled the stick back, but the plane continued to fall. With the wind whistling through the flying wires, he tinkered with the controls, but to no avail — the plane was going down. Finally, he pushed the throttle all the way forward, holding full back on the stick. There was a church steeple about even with him just off to the left, when the nose of the plane pulled up and he began to climb.

Barr experimented with the controls on the way back to Detroit, and found he could keep the plane flying evenly only with the throttle wide open. As he headed south in helmet and goggles with the engine roaring, Barr lined up to land on the long paved runway at the municipal airport. He began the descent a long way out, skimming over houses and factories as he inched downward in the speeding plane. The gravestones in a cemetery at the end of the runway flashed beneath his wheels. He cut the throttle. The plane touched the ground, and rolled all the way to the end of the airstrip. It may have been the fastest landing ever made in an airplane of that type.

"I climbed out of the cockpit with rubbery legs and sweaty hands, and faced a small group of pilots and mechanics demanding to know just what kind of damned fool I was, flying down the runway like that, endangering all the planes lined up on the ramp," he said.

After checking the plane out, Barr concluded it needed a larger stabilizer. In level flight, air flow over the stabilizer normally acts to keep the tail down, counteracting the engine's extra weight in the nose of the plane. He got a bigger stabilizer off an old Waco and went "hunting" no more in the Pheasant.

He did plenty of flying in it though, and often cruised over Detroit on warm summer nights carrying passengers or freight. The plane was eventually grounded for good when an inspector found the steel frame was so rusted in spots that his penknife went right through it.

"I had lots of confidence in those days," Barr said years later. "Today I wouldn't even get in that airplane if it was on the ground, much less fly across the city of Detroit at night."

Barr's freight on those night flights was often illegal booze he was importing from Canada. Prohibition was on at that time and since the mile-wide Detroit River was the only thing standing between the city and good Canadian whiskey, Barr picked up a few bucks bootlegging.

Detroit was the automotive capital of the world, but as the *New York Times* reported, "There are imposing and reasonably reliable figures to support the statement that the illegal liquor business is Detroit's second largest industry." Most bootlegging into the "Rum Capital" was done by speedboat across the river from Windsor, Ontario. The liquor flowed like water into the 25,000 illegal saloons, or "blind pigs," where Detroit's thirsty could get a beer for a quarter. Barr said he did not consider bootlegging a crime and public opinion was generally in his favor. Detroit's mayor of the time campaigned against "fanaticism," which was taken to mean enforcement of the liquor laws.

For a while Barr got $50 a flight from a Canadian who hired him to pilot a J-5 Waco that could hold twenty cases of liquor. He thought of it as a game in which the object was to beat the border patrol. He'd fly over the border and land in a farmer's field on the U.S. side, where a car would be waiting to pick up the cargo. The driver would put out a signal if there was a strange car around, or if it wasn't safe to land. The unloading crew would do its job in one minute and drive away with the cargo. Then Barr would taxi to the end of the field and take off.

"I really thought I was doing a service to the people by supplying them with first-quality booze, instead of that rotgut they had to buy sometimes."

He had one close call with the J-5 Waco, when he landed in a small dirt field near Detroit and broke a wheel. The ground crew unloaded the liquor and Barr went looking for a new wheel for the crippled plane. Before the authorities could find the plane, he scavenged a wheel designed for a lighter aircraft and flew back to Canada. The wire wheel gave way just when he pulled into the hangar and the plane "knelt down like a tired old hen."

Another way to fly for money that was even more dangerous than bootlegging, was test flying for various backyard inventors. Some of these would-be manufacturers had radical ideas and no money — a hazardous or comical combination. One such inventor Barr knew had built an airplane out of angle iron with some kind of patent leather over the wings. Barr watched as the owner wheeled it out, put on his helmet, and prepared for the checkout ride in the iron bird.

"He adjusted everything perfectly, then he opened the throttle wide and the airplane just sat there. One fellow standing by took hold of the trailing edge of the rudder and pushed it a little and the plane rolled ahead ten feet and stopped."

Barr even tried some backyard building, himself, going in with several friends in the purchase of plans for a wooden plane that they called the "Gaspipe Special." He flew it five times and had five forced landings.

One day Barr saw a newspaper story that an airplane owned by Cain Aircraft had spun into the ground, killing the test pilot. Barr applied to fill the dead man's shoes and test-flew a second plane which had been redesigned to correct the balance problem that had killed the pilot. Barr also did some flying for A.S. Barkley, who built a good all-metal airplane with two long booms to the rear and vertical fins.

Barkley told the newspapers that a three-foot hole could be shot through the plane's honeycomb-like wings without reducing their strength. He had worked on the plane for seventeen years and he hoped to sell it to the Army for use as a light, fast pursuit plane.

Barr flew the plane at Wayne County Airport near Detroit in May, 1931, at a session attended by news photographers and others whom Barkley had invited to see his "Flying Wing."

Barr thought Barkley's mistake was that he kept tinkering with the plane's design. Barr had to take a trip to Toronto, and while he was gone, Barkley added another gas tank at the rear and got another pilot to fly the plane. The gas tank made the plane tail heavy and it spun into the ground, killing the pilot.

Another of Barr's test-pilot jobs was with E.P. Hurd, a small, chunky man who owned an automobile lock factory and had taken up building planes as a hobby. With about 150 hours' flying time in his log book, Barr was considered an experienced pilot by this time.

Hurd's first plane was a beauty, Barr said, a two-seat open plane with thick, low wings. It did have a problem Hurd's engineer did not forsee, though: It was too heavy to take off. As Hurd later joked to Barr over the fiasco, "This is a revolutionary airplane. The payload is built right in." Hurd hired a new engineer to change the design and Barr was soon ready to take it up for a test ride.

On his first hop in Hurd's HM-1 monoplane, everything went fine. It had a sixty-horsepower Le Blond engine and it handled well and had good control, although the cruising speed of eighty-five miles per hour was considered slow even then. It was the spin test required by the Department of Commerce that nearly cost Barr his life when he next took the plane up. They had gone out to a vacant field to do the test before the eyes of a government inspector. The object was to establish that the plane could be put into a spin and come out of it without killing the pilot.

"Well, I chopped the throttle, pulled the nose up into a stall, and kicked the rudder full over. It dropped away easily into a spin, but then things started happening in a confused mess. The tail dropped so low that the fuselage was nearly horizontal. The rate of rotation was so great, the ground was only a blur. "I didn't feel the rush of air against my face. It was as if there was no forward movement at all, just a settling straight down as the plane whipped around." He became instantly nauseous and said he didn't give a damn whether it ever came out of that spin or not.

"The stick was 'way back in my belly and I was trying to push it forward, but I didn't have the strength. Then I thought, 'I've got to do this some way,' so I started working the throttle and the stick together and rocking it a little bit, and pretty soon she tipped over and came out."

He straightened out the plane at 1,000 feet and slumped down in the seat, feeling sick to his stomach. Hurd and his engineer told Barr later that he was spinning so fast they couldn't get an accurate count, but he had gone around at least thirty times.

"I've been awful lucky that way," Barr recalled. "I can think of at least eight or nine times that I could have cracked up but didn't."

The engineer went back to the drawing board, moved the wings back a few inches to change the center of gravity, and the problem was solved.

He had another misadventure with the plane when flying over Troy, New York, and his engine suddenly quit. Barr found out later that the crankshaft had broken, but at that time he only knew he had to land in an orchard near the Hudson River. He went down between two rows of old apple trees and that sheared off the wings. The propeller broke off and sailed away, but the pilot was uninjured.

He rolled to a stop and was thinking what a mess he was in, when the breathless farmer came out to see what had happened. The farmer could not believe that Barr was uninjured. After assuring the farmer for the third time that he was OK, Barr asked, "Is this your first airplane accident?"

Barr helped rebuild the plane and returned to Detroit, where in 1931 he got wind of a gold expedition being put together for the Yukon Territory.

The organizer was a persuasive man named Tom Mitchell, who said he had found a rich gold strike and needed investors and partners to develop it. Mitchell's tale was a fantastic one and he carried several nuggets with him to back up his claim. He said he and a partner had discovered gold, but the partner had died and he had struggled back to civilization alone. Now he had come to Detroit and was walking the streets, trying to sell a vision of a new Klondike during the Great Depression. It sounded too good to be true. It was.

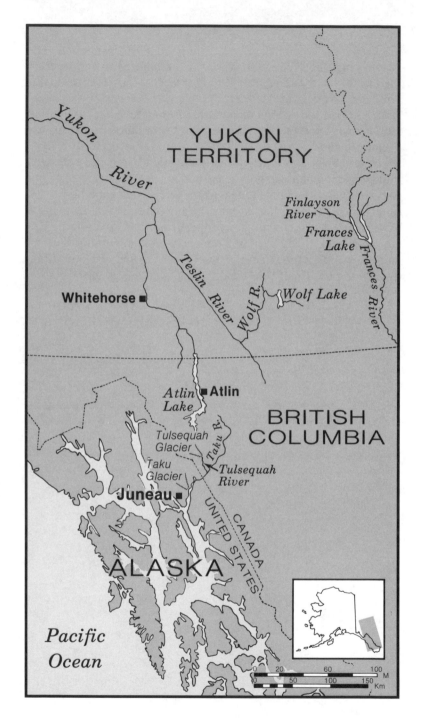

CHAPTER 5

The Mitchell Drinking Expedition

Thomas M. MITCHELL didn't try to convince Detroit's businessmen that the Yukon was paved with gold. He just said he knew of creeks that were. A rugged-looking man who had spent his life outdoors, Mitchell was a crack shot with a pistol and a smooth talker who hit the bull's-eye with his tales of gold.

It was the cruelest year of the Depression and in a city where dreams of prosperity had succumbed to soup lines and idle factories, the idea of digging a fortune out of the ground was irresistible.

"Tom was not your run-of-the-mill promoter," Barr said. "He was not a large, bluff, fast talking man — just the opposite. He gave the appearance of being rather shrewd and when he talked of his gold prospect, he gave you the impression that he was holding something back."

What he told his prospective investors about his gold discovery seemed plausible enough; he didn't want to stake one claim for himself and let the rest go to strangers. Instead, he needed money to organize a company of prospectors to stake a large area.

"We expect to put experienced men in the field and keep them there," Mitchell told a reporter. "We will grubstake them for the summer and maintain them there on a fifty-fifty basis on their entire cleanup. Nothing, I am sure, could be fairer to the prospector than that."

Mitchell's plans captured the imaginations of several key people in the Detroit area. One of them was James Eastman, thirty-six, a respected dental equipment manufacturer who had, in the late

1920s, built a flying boat called the Eastman Flying Yacht. Eastman had merged his company into a conglomerate called Detroit Aircraft, but the venture collapsed during the Depression.

The owners of the *Detroit News* were interested as well. The newspaper sent a plane to the Far North in March, 1932, to check out the gold potential. *Detroit News* pilot Frank Byerly flew Mitchell, Eastman and three others in the newspaper's Lockheed Vega to the Liard placer district in the southeast part of the Yukon. They landed on the ice of Frances Lake and walked a short distance up the Finlayson River. The snow prevented a detailed examination of the gold claim, but the flying prospectors dug down and found "colors" at a site identified by Mitchell as some 275 miles northeast of Juneau.

The thrill of finding a little gold silenced the skeptics, and the survey party flashed the green light to Detroit. "The report of this survey smoothed out the financing," Mitchell said. Within weeks the Mitchell Exploration Company, Ltd., had raised between $75,000 and $150,000 for its aerial assault on the gold fields, the *Alaska Daily Empire* of Juneau reported.

The five remaining Eastman Flying Yachts became the backbone of the operation. Eastman, who was named vice president of Mitchell Exploration, flew one ship, and he was joined by four veteran pilots.

One was Red Harrigan, who had served in the Navy for about twenty years and was the chief test pilot for Ryan Aircraft in California. At that time Harrigan had crossed the Rocky Mountains fifty-four times by plane, a record. He said later that when he flew over the mountain range in the Eastman Flying Yacht, it was the first time he had done so in a plane equipped with an anchor, life preserver and oars.

The other pilots included Byerly of the *Detroit News,* D.M. Emery, a former wing commander in the Royal Air Force, and E.C. Burton, a former airmail pilot who flew for years at night between Ottawa and Detroit.

The five flying boats left Walkerville, Ontario, on May 25, 1932, carrying the leaders of the Mitchell expedition and as much equipment as they could cram aboard. The planes, which could cruise at ninety miles per hour, followed the route of the Canadian National Railway as they hopped across the continent with Byerly leading the way. They reached the coast, turned north, and arrived in Juneau, Alaska's capital, in sixteen days.

In Juneau they met several other expedition members who had

One of the five "Eastman Flying Yachts" that the "Drinking Expedition" took north to Juneau in 1932, preparing to take off on ice from Atlin.

come by rail and ship. By now the prospecting party had swollen to thirty-five men, including an assortment of millionaires and laborers, a legal adviser, a representative of the *Detroit News,* a mining engineer and a twenty-eight-year-old former calvalryman, parachute jumper and test pilot named Frank Barr.

Barr had hoped to fly one of the planes when he first heard about the expedition, but Eastman already had a full crew. So Barr came along as a prospector and backup pilot. The Depression had put the test pilot business into a tailspin and he had nothing to lose. Barr took a train to Prince Rupert and sailed in steerage on the *Princess Nora* through the fjords of Southeast Alaska.

He was down to eight dollars when he stepped off the boat in Juneau, a compact town squeezed onto a small shelf of land beneath 3,600-foot Mount Juneau. He found that the Eastman Expedition was the talk of the town. Some of the members were already counting their money before they even got to the gold fields.

"As is usual when any considerable number of men band together to go into any new mining area, many 'stampede' rumors have been in circulation here for several days," the Juneau newspaper reported June 11. "Stories of a rich strike, all of which have failed of confirmation, have been whispered, 'out of one hole, enough gold was washed in a single day to pay for one of the planes,' was one 'true' version of the origin of the expedition. Others were more conservative, but still highly flavored and all to the effect that another Klondike was in the making."

In the midst of this wild talk, Juneau outfitters sold out of gold pans and there was a heavy run on bedrolls, mosquito netting, and "everything that the well-financed prospector ought to wear and have." At least two other groups made arrangements to fly to the Liard district to compete with Mitchell's party.

One group was led by "Stampede" John Stenbraten, a well-known prospector who was said to have participated in every gold rush in the English-speaking world during his lifetime. His custom was to run to the new gold diggings as soon as the news broke. "We shall have our stakes in the ground by tonight," Stenbraten told a reporter before leaving Juneau.

The other competitor was Vern Gorst, who had pioneered airmail service on the West Coast in 1926. The Juneau headlines said, "Air Stampede Starts from here for Liard," and everyone was optimistic for a time.

Mitchell did nothing to cool the gold fever in Juneau, but his public statements showed more reserve than the glowing reports he had issued in Detroit. He told the Juneau newspaper he was enthusiastic, and in a general way spoke of thousands of creeks waiting to be explored.

"I know of several rich spots we shall work at once," he announced. "There is enough of this ground to keep a dozen outfits like ours going for many years."

Mitchell said he had made aerial surveys of Alaska, the Yukon and northern British Columbia in 1929 and 1930, and the expedition would examine the richer spots he had found.

The planes flew up the Taku River to Tulsequah, where 5,000 gallons of gas had been purchased, and then on into Atlin, B.C., before going northeast to the gold fields.

A.M. Smith, a representative of the *Detroit News,* gave a progress report on the expedition during a visit to Juneau in early July. "Placer gold in minute particles is found quite generally in the creeks. To discover gold of coarser character is a task that requires organized effort and patience. The Mitchell party is exerting the one and has the other," Smith said.

By that time, pilot Red Harrigan had been called back to Ryan Aircraft in California. It was a lucky break for Barr, who replaced Harrigan at the controls of one of the Eastman flying boats, ferrying supplies to Frances Lake from the base camp at Atlin, a small gold mining town on ninety-mile-long Atlin Lake. In later years, Barr always referred to the gold-hunting group as the "Mitchell Drinking Expedition" because of the increase in liquor sales at Atlin after its arrival.

The flights from Atlin to Frances Lake were made difficult by the limitations of the four-seat Eastman planes, which were basically designed for sport flying and were supposed to carry a load of 980 pounds. The planes carried so little cargo, Barr said, that the pilot could either "carry freight and stay there or carry extra gas and get back."

They set up camp on Frances Lake at a sandy beach near where there had once been a Hudson's Bay post. While the pilots were hauling in supplies, Harry Townsend, a prominent Seattle mining engineer hired by the expedition, surveyed the gold prospects. After a painstaking search of several areas, he issued his verdict in late July. It was not what the expedition wanted to hear: Mitchell's bonanza was worth only one or two cents a pan.

It wouldn't pay to travel three miles to find this deposit, much less three thousand, and the expedition members felt they had been conned. The gold boom which Mitchell said would last years was over before it began.

C.O. Butcher, a wealthy Detroit contractor and one of Mitchell's principal backers, told a reporter the only reason they came was that they believed a proven gold strike had been discovered.

"If the project had been understood as merely a prospecting trip, many of us would not have undertaken it," Butcher said.

When the word of the fiasco spread, Mitchell's stock dropped to zero and he was deposed as expedition leader. Eastman was not a violent man, but he became angry enough to pick a fight with Mitchell in Atlin.

"Eastman got the worst of it," said Ted Burton, a lawyer in Ontario whose father, expedition pilot Ed Burton, was a witness to the affair. In 1979 he wrote Barr about his father's adventure.

"Mitchell chewed on Eastman's thumb and a doctor had to sew it up. When Eastman came out of the anesthetic he was in great pain, and the doctor asked Pop to keep him quiet because he had an emergency in the next room. Pop told Eastman he had done a real number on Mitchell (which wasn't true, he only gave him a black eye) and Eastman got so excited he shook the bloody bandages off his hand," Ted Burton said.

"It was the following day that Mitchell went south," Burton's son remembered. "I believe Pop told me that it was simply a matter of telling the local Mountie the whole story and they invited Mitchell to leave town, which he prudently did."

A half-century after the expedition folded its tent, it's still not clear what exactly Mitchell's game was. Barr had heard that it wasn't the first nor the last mining promotion he had pulled. Perhaps Mitchell hoped the "colors" he had found would be enough to string the Detroit group along until they actually found something.

In any case, by the time Mitchell was dumped, most of the gold hunters wanted nothing more to do with the Far North. Barr said he tried to get them to leave their supplies of rice, flour, sugar and oatmeal at Frances Lake to grubstake a few old-time prospectors who had become his friends, but the others refused.

He got angry and took the distributor rotor off the plane that was going to leave with the supplies, but Barr had no time to plan his next move. Byerly walked over to where Barr was sitting, bowled him over, and went through his pockets until he found the missing rotor. At that point one of the expedition members pulled a gun on Barr, but he was talked out of using it.

No one made any money to speak of from the Drinking Expedition, but it wasn't a total washout for Barr, nor for Eastman. Barr liked the North and decided to stay, ending that summer with a firm conviction that he'd make his living in the air, not in the ground.

"When others talked about all the gold," he said, "all I could see was the gravel."

Eastman's was a different story. He eventually found the gold he had sought and became a successful and respected miner in the Atlin area. He continued to fly and helped many people on mercy missions over the years. When he needed help the most, however, there was no one to give it. According to Atlin old-timers he died in 1945, of appendicitis, because there was no one to fly him to the hospital in Whitehorse. He is buried in Atlin, in a grave marked by the propeller of an old plane.

CHAPTER 6

Adventures in Atlin

THE MITCHELL EXPEDITION may have been a failure in more ways than one, but it succeeded in proving the advantages of the airplane to Bill Strong, who had shipped gasoline and other supplies up the Taku River for Mitchell.

Strong had a trading post at Tulsequah, about forty miles from Juneau, and he had spent enough years slogging through the muskeg and pushing boats against the current to recognize an improvement when he saw it.

In the spring of 1933 he sent Barr to Seattle to pick up a used Fokker Flying Boat he had purchased from airmail pioneer and prospector Vern Gorst.

The plane came with an advertised top speed of 112 miles per hour, but Barr figured its actual speed was closer to 70 miles per hour. The plane had a double aluminum hull for landing on water, and a Hornet engine mounted on four legs above the fuselage. It could carry a big load of freight or nine passengers. "It wasn't much of an airplane, but it was a wonderful boat," Barr said. "I had occasion to land it right out in the ocean once or twice, and I'll tell you it could take it."

The three-bladed prop made a terrific noise and people in Juneau used to joke that you could hear him coming yesterday if he arrived today. George Robbins, who lived in Atlin at the time and worked for Strong, told Barr it was a thrill to hear him take off from Atlin Lake.

"It seemed a good thing the lake was one hundred miles long, and sometimes it looked as if you were going to use every bit of it."

Bill Strong's Fokker Flying Boat, at Atlin, British Columbia, in 1933. Frank Barr is sitting on the hull holding a paddle. "It wasn't much of an airplane," Barr said of the Fokker, "but it was a wonderful boat." The three-bladed prop was so noisy, people in Juneau used to joke that you could hear Barr coming yesterday if he arrived today.

Barr and the big flying boat soon became a common sight in the little mining town.

Atlin, which had a population of about three hundred in the winter and twice that in the summer, was actually an offshoot of the Klondike gold rush. Two men from Juneau, Fritz Miller and Kenny McLaren, struck gold there in July, 1898. Soon there was a bustling town of five thousand, with a newspaper, three churches, three banks, three real estate companies and a curling rink. The gold boom ended by 1908, but mining kept the town alive.

Like many former gold-rush towns, Atlin survived in a setting of beauty and isolation that has changed little. Snow-covered

mountains reflect in a mirror image on the deep blue lake, which is still clean enough to supply the town's drinking water. In the Coast Mountains fifty miles to the west, the thousand-square-mile Juneau icecap feeds Taku Glacier, Mendenhall Glacier and thirty others.

"Name any resort and this is just as pretty," author Edward Hoagland wrote after a visit to Atlin in the 1960s. "Yet horses graze down the street, fireweed grows in the vacant lots, loons and sea gulls swim up to the shore."

It was not much different in the 1930s. A road did not reach Atlin until 1949. Before then the main transportation link was by boat across Atlin and Tagish lakes to Carcross, a stop on the White Pass and Yukon Route Railroad.

Isolated from the rest of the world, the people of Atlin were a closely knit group. When Barr arrived on the scene, a provincial policeman, a government liquor vendor and a government agent were the authority figures in town.

Clarence Sands, an Englishman who had fought in the Boer War, ran a clothing store and also sold English china and yard goods, cosmetics, etcetera. He had come to Atlin when gold was at its peak, and stayed.

Another who did likewise was Jim Kershaw, who ran the hardware store. He told Barr that when he had walked overland from Telegraph Creek during the gold boom, he encountered many unfortunate victims of con artists. Four days out of Telegraph Creek, he and his partner ran into three young men carrying nothing to eat but vitamin pills. They had been convinced by a fast-talking salesman that the pills would supply all of their nutritional needs and that they'd be relieved of the necessity of carrying heavy food.

The gold rush which had brought the ravenous greenhorns to the North was a dim memory when Barr heard the story, but even in 1933 there were enough prospectors and trappers in the region to keep the Fokker busy.

On July 18 Barr was bound for Strong's headquarters at Tulsequah, on the Taku River near the border with Alaska, when the noisy engine went silent. Although the landing conditions were marginal, he turned and managed to land upstream in a long, narrow valley.

The river in that area is navigable only by small boats and there were no communications facilities, so no one knew Barr was missing. He couldn't walk to Tulsequah because the river came up against a steep limestone cliff in two places and the ground was covered with dense underbrush, so he camped on the river near the plane and waited, living off his ample supplies of emergency rations.

His plane was spotted several days later by Jim Eastman, who was flying up the Taku toward Atlin. After circling overhead to make sure Barr was not injured, Eastman continued to Atlin and sent a telegram to Juneau giving Barr's location.

A couple of days later word filtered upstream to Strong, who loaded his boat with tools and a couple of helpers and went after Barr.

When he found Barr eight days after the forced landing and looked the plane over, Strong joked, "Didn't you have a match?"

But instead of burning the plane to collect the insurance, they loaded the engine into Strong's boat and began the difficult task of guiding the Fokker downstream. They had to stop frequently to cut sweepers — downed trees lying partly across the river — and to get over snags which would have torn the plane apart in the

Barr made a forced landing on the upper Taku River in 1933. He waited eight days until Bill Strong arrived with a boat, and they dismantled the engine and towed the wrecked Fokker downstream.

swift current. The engine had to be sent to Vancouver for repairs, and Barr began flying a World War I Moth biplane that Strong had bought.

As summer turned to fall and the hours of daylight and the temperature decreased, Barr stayed warm in the open cockpit plane by wearing a flying suit which smelled like dog fur and weighed about thirty pounds. On several occasions he bundled up in the suit and made mail trips to the Norgold Mine. There was no landing strip there, so he had to improvise. The bag of outgoing mail would be strung up on a rope and Barr would fly by, drop down a hook, and lift the bag into the plane, then drop the incoming mail and head back to town.

In November he took off on his trip to Wolf Lake, where the storm flipped the airplane and grounded him for six weeks. He returned to Atlin in January, with a banged up plane and no place to repair it. When they heard of his plight, Bill and Aunty Roxborough, owners of Atlin's Kootenay Hotel, agreed to let Barr work on the plane in the hotel lobby. Airplanes were still regarded as a wonder of the age, and people went out of their way to be of assistance.

A big barrel stove kept the lobby warm and Barr spread the damaged wing over the pool table. The lobby still smelled from the nitro-cellulose dope he'd spread over the new wing fabric, when the Atlin telegraph operator received an urgent call for help from the south.

The SOS came from a former telegraph lineman and trapper who had cut his foot with an ax and crawled to the telegraph line to tap out an emergency message. He had lost a lot of blood and needed medical attention immediately.

Barr quickly reassembled the Moth, the only plane within hundreds of miles, and took off the next morning at daylight. He stopped for fuel on Sawmill Lake and as he poured gas into the tank from the extra cans he carried in the cockpit, he was stunned by what he saw when he looked the plane over. A nut was missing on a bolt which held the flying wires and the wings in place. If the air hadn't been exceptionally smooth on the way down, the bolt would have been knocked out and the wings would have collapsed.

Without a word to the small group of people who had gathered to watch him refuel, Barr found a nut in his tool kit and corrected the problem. He had always taken great pride in his mechanical work, but more than his ego would have been damaged, had the wings come off in flight.

He continued south to pick up the injured trapper, wrapped him

When Barr and mechanic Jess Rice formed North Canada Air Express in about 1934, the first plane they purchased was a Model S Stinson. The plane was a workhorse, but couldn't carry a big load. On this particular spring day, one ski went through the ice of Atlin Lake.

Changing Barr's Stinson from skis to floats at Atlin in 1934. The Stinson was the first airplane Barr owned, and his log books show that he made 247 flights in the plane.

in two sleeping bags, and delivered him to a nurse at Telegraph Creek on the Stikine River.

The trapper recovered from his foot injury, but Barr wondered later whether the mercy mission had been a mistake. Some years after recovering from the accident, the trapper, in a drunken rage, shot a man to death in Atlin.

Barr flew for Strong for a couple of years, but the trader eventually pulled the plug on the operation because it wasn't making any money. Barr then decided to buy his own plane and start a flying business with mechanic Jess Rice.

As usual he had no money, but this time he knew where to get it.

"I went around and mined all the miners," he said. "They all recognized the need for an airplane in Atlin."

Barr bought a used model S Stinson in Saskatchewan, and flew back to Atlin in the only asset of a company he and Rice called North Canada Air Express. Barr began wearing a captain's hat with gold braid and the company name on the front of it. He wore the hat for years before, one day on a flight in Alaska to Ruby, he stuck his head out the window and the hat sailed off onto the tundra.

The Stinson was a good old workhorse, but operating off Atlin Lake, at an altitude of 2,200 feet, it couldn't carry a big load.

"In the wintertime I could take off with two passengers and baggage pretty well. On skis I had the whole lake to take off from. But if the lake was just a little bit rough in the summertime you couldn't do that," Barr said. "Not on floats."

He flew to Carcross to meet the White Pass Railroad, and to Whitehorse, Teslin, the Norgold Mine, and many other spots in northern British Columbia and the Yukon.

Barr's log books list 247 flights with the Stinson, but he rarely recorded the names of his passengers along with the flight statistics — where he went and how long it took. He had good reason, however, to write down the names of geologist Joseph Mandy and his wife, Madge, after he took them on a two-and-a-half-hour trip to McDames, on the Dease River, on June 29, 1935.

It was Barr's first flight to McDames Post and he was fighting a strong headwind all the way from Atlin. According to his gas gauge he still had enough fuel left for twenty minutes of flight, when the engine quit and he had to land on the river. It was one flight Barr would never forget. Neither did his passengers. Forty-six years later Mrs. Mandy wrote to him:

"You made so many flights in the North that you probably do not recall taking Dr. Mandy and me from Atlin to McDames Post on the Dease River. I never knew why we ran out of gas, but I will never forget your calmness and skill in landing on the water when aware of the problem."

Madge remembered that when the plane landed, Barr turned around and said, "Most people think when you run out of gas in the air, you die. But you see, you don't."

She said, "Your words certainly put us at ease as well as your quiet and philosophical acceptance of the situation."

Then the three of them turned the Stinson into a riverboat to cover the last few miles.

"You sat on one pontoon, using the only ax on board, and Dr. Mandy on the other pontoon put an ax handle to use." Madge wrote. "I sat at the controls, following instructions which you called out to me. Our main problem was to keep in midstream to avoid sweeping tree branches on the riverbanks."

As they floated downstream, Barr explained that he would be a disgrace among pilots, once they learned what had happened. Worse yet, it would scare off passengers.

Joseph Mandy told Barr he had nothing to worry about; he and his wife would never tell anyone what happened that day on the river. When people at McDames Post asked why the plane was floating instead of flying, Mandy replied that Barr had put the Stinson down because they had spotted a rock formation that deserved a closer look. Mandy added that they were just a short distance upstream, so they decided to save gas and float the rest of the way.

After that flight, Barr never again trusted the gas gauge on his Stinson, and he never again ran out of gas in twenty-five years of flying.

The secret was still safe in 1979 when Madge, a former drama coach and college speech professor, asked Barr whether she could use the story in her memoirs.

"Like my husband, I do not wish to cause you any embarrassment, even at this late date," she wrote. "Possibly there are no people in Atlin or the Cassiar who would remember our unusual journey. I could get a good effect by saying some problem developed which I did not understand that made landing on the river advisable.

"On the other hand, I should like to give credit to you as one of the best pilots the North ever had, who never allowed anything to seemingly disturb you."

Frank Barr and his Pilgrim at the Juneau Airport in the mid-1930s. (Ray Robinson Collection)

CHAPTER 7

A Shoestring Operation

IN FRANK BARR'S case, the toughest part of flying had nothing to do with piloting an airplane. It was his attitude toward book-keeping that always threatened to put an end to his one-plane company.

"The real problem was, I was not a businessman. I just wanted to fly, and I would arrange things so I could fly. If somebody couldn't afford to pay, I'd work out a deal — trade something or give them a cut rate or whatever, just so I could fly."

If they weren't getting rich with that attitude, Barr and Rice were at least generating more traffic than they could possibly handle with the Stinson. Barr flew everything from bales of hay and powder puffs to groceries and prospectors throughout the Yukon, Southeast Alaska and northern British Columbia.

Needing a bigger airplane to keep up with the demand, they went down to Dallas, Texas, in October, 1935, and bought a used Pilgrim monoplane from American Airlines for $3,000. The fabric was tattered, but the engine was in good shape.

On the return trip to Atlin with the new plane, Barr and Rice were waylaid at Boeing Field by a reporter from the *Seattle Times*. Barr, wearing a leather flying jacket, a tie and his "North Canada Air Express" pilot's hat, didn't want to make the wrong impression.

"Barr smiled yesterday when interviewed and said he was ashamed to be caught working," the reporter wrote.

Pleasantries aside, the reporter figured that Barr and Rice were doing pretty well for a couple of young men starting out in business.

"Of course, there are a few details of northern flying that keep the business from growing boresome," he wrote. "There are no beacons out in the frozen wastes. There are no radio beams and few weather stations. A pilot just takes up a ship and looks around. If things seem all right, he flies. If a storm comes up, he turns back or 'sits down.' "

Barr recounted a few war stories of forced landings and breakdowns and added that insurance companies were cynical about flying in the North. Buying insurance for their plane, which was one of the largest in the North at that time, would run about one-quarter of the Pilgrim's cost for one year's coverage, the newspaper said.

It may have been expensive to insure, but it was a joy to fly. Barr liked the big Pilgrim more than any other plane he ever flew. It offered great visibility and was a real workhorse.

The five-foot, seven-inch pilot sat nearly ten feet off the ground in an enclosed single-seat cockpit. Unlike some planes, in which the engine blocked the view, the Pilgrim was designed so the pilot could see over the power plant.

The Pilgrim could pack 2,000 pounds of cargo or nine passengers and it flew well in all kinds of weather. It was the first plane to be steam-heated. The factory said it could cruise at 110 miles per hour, but the actual speed was more like 98 miles per hour.

Barr's Pilgrim may have been a little rough looking when he bought it, but with meticulous maintenance and constant care, the plane served him well for many years of heavy use in wild country. "I landed it many times where you shouldn't land an airplane," he said.

Although it was well-equipped for passengers, with reclining seats, overhead baggage racks and a toilet, the Pilgrim was not a commercial success for Fairchild Aircraft and fewer than twenty were built. The American public was still wary of flying in the 1930s, and a plane with one man in the cockpit and one engine did not compare favorably with multi-engine planes with two pilots.

In Alaska, however, the plane won many converts and Pilgrims were flown by Pan American, Harold Gillam, Alaska Airlines and others. Pan Am turned out to be a good source of used parts for Barr in later years. A big company like that could afford to throw away parts that were worn, but not worn out. Barr said the tires and other parts always looked brand new on his Pilgrim when he salvaged them from Pan Am's junk pile.

"I was operating on a shoestring," Barr liked to say, "Sort of a worn and frayed shoestring."

The city of Juneau from across Gastineau Channel.

A pilot's view of Atlin, British Columbia, on the shores of Atlin Lake in about 1935. Barr arrived in Atlin in 1932 with the Mitchell gold hunting expedition, and became one of the first bush pilots to be based in the town.

With the arrival of the Pilgrim, Barr tried to establish regular service between Atlin and Juneau and he memorized the hundred-mile ice-capped route. First he had to overcome a big obstacle on flights to Juneau; he had no landing field.

The grass-covered tide flats outside of Juneau, which were exposed at low tide, proved to be an acceptable alternative. Today Boeing 727s land on a modern paved runway nearby, but in those days Barr just used the grass flats. He always carried a tide book in the cockpit.

"It would be embarrassing to come down from Atlin and find that the tide was in," he said. He wasn't permitted to use the landing field Pan Am had built for its Lockheed Electras, which flew to Whitehorse and Fairbanks.

If Pan Am didn't welcome Barr with open arms, neither did the White Pass Railroad. The narrow-gauge rail line, which operated for more than eighty years between Skagway and Whitehorse, was a mainstay in the empire of the White Pass, the company that once ruled Whitehorse in the Yukon Territory.

Aside from the railroad, the company operated riverboats to Dawson, a stage line and, later, an airline. White Pass was run by H.J. Wheeler, a fighting Irishman known as "Old One-eye" who operated like an old cattle baron of the West.

Barr remembered a placard at Lake Bennett, a railroad stop about halfway between Skagway and Whitehorse. The sign said that if any of the company's competitors had a forced landing along their rail line, no employee was to give the downed flier any assistance.

In *Bush Pilot With a Briefcase,* pilot Grant McConachie, a competitor of White Pass, told of his first encounter with Wheeler.

"I want to tell you something, young man," Wheeler said. "I'm going to run you out of this country." Asked why, the White Pass chief replied, "You know damn well why. We came in here. There was nothing. White Pass built this country from nothing. Lost a few fortunes doing it. Mail, passenger, cargo; it's our business here. There's no place for an upstart like you."

"Old One-eye" undoubtedly felt the same way about Barr, but North Canada Air Express persisted against the not-too-friendly competition.

Writing in 1978 about the time he flew from Juneau to Atlin with Barr, Bob McCombe recalled that most of the passengers were worried as they flew over the ice field in the moonlight.

"As we approached that lake, I must hand it to Mr. Barr. He made no false passes. He came in and landed on that ice just like he was

*Frank Barr's Pilgrim could carry 2,000 pounds of cargo or nine passengers.
"I landed it many times where you shouldn't land an airplane," Barr said.
He is unloading freight here on the Tulsequah River for a nearby mine.*

---

landing on La Guardia Field in New York, and of course everybody
in town rushed out to greet the plane . . ."

The ice field near Juneau has the scenery of "a dozen flights rolled
into one," a writer who dubbed Barr the "Ice Cap Pilot" said in 1938,
but at times it's the source of savage winds.

The Taku winds were blowing the day Barr left Juneau with two
miners who were returning home to Atlin. When they were flying
through the choppy air, the lid came off a five-gallon milk can in
front of the miners, and they were wearing the milk, not drinking it.

Barr occasionally ran into rough weather and mechanical
problems, but most of the time passengers couldn't tell the difference
between a dangerous situation and a run-of-the-mill flight. While
taking a load of freight and a lone Atlin prospector named Matthews
home from Juneau, Barr's motor started blowing oil all over the
windshield as he flew up the Taku River. Barr didn't know exactly
what the problem was, but he knew it wasn't good. He headed back
to Juneau.

The windshield was opaque from the oil and he had to look out
the side window to see when he reached the grassy flats.

Blissfully unaware of what had just happened, his passenger
thought the lack of visibility was due to fog. "Well, the weather
is pretty bad, maybe we'll make it the next time," Matthews said.

Then there were occasions when the pilot didn't know what he was getting into. Barr once flew Vern "Pop" Gorst, a miner and pilot, to Juneau in the Pilgrim. The weather was beautiful in Atlin, but it kept getting worse and worse the farther he went down the Taku River. Barr decided to play it safe and land on what appeared to be a nice soft swamp behind Mary Joyce's Lodge on the bank of the river.

What looked like short green grass turned out to be soft muck with a green scum on top. The airplane dug two deep tracks and rolled to a stop, nosing over in the ooze. Neither man was injured and the plane was undamaged. As they climbed out they sank up to their knees in muck. Trudging through the slime toward Mary Joyce's Lodge, Barr found a great patch of huckleberries. He started running his fingers through the bush and picking out big handfuls.

"Well, my God," said Gorst, "I never saw anybody so enthused over berries before, right after a forced landing."

The berries were new to Barr. The forced landings were not. Later he got help from Juneau and they propped up the plane, put skis on and took off through the swamp.

Mary Joyce, at whose lodge Barr often stopped, came to Alaska in 1930. After quitting a job in a Hollywood hospital, she accompanied a wealthy family as their nurse on a boating trip to Alaska, and decided to stay.

In 1936 she was named Miss Juneau, and along with a guide, she drove a dog team more than one thousand miles to participate in the ice carnival in Fairbanks. It took her 52 days to get to Tanacross. She flew the rest of the way to Fairbanks to make it in time for the contest. She didn't win the Miss Alaska title, but she returned to Tanacross and mushed her dogs the rest of the way to Fairbanks.

Her lodge on the Taku River was a popular resort, with a main building where the guests ate their meals near a big, open fireplace. In the winter of 1936 Barr was forced to spend the last three weeks of December at the lodge, because of the lack of reliable weather reports.

There was no snow in Atlin when he took off for Juneau, but the weather closed in on him and he landed on wheels near a barn built by an old farmer named Bullard. He walked back to Mary Joyce's place to wait for better weather. The snow fell for days, and he could do little but shovel it off the plane.

Barr had left the plane's skis back in Atlin, so he built a temporary set out of some old barn planks. The new skis weren't fancy, just practical. They looked like window boxes with one end open, and they were fitted under the wheels.

The idea was that the skis would stay on the ground when the wheels lifted off. When the snow finally stopped he spent several hard days stamping out an 800-foot runway with his snowshoes. He hoped to get up enough speed so he could ride up on top of the loose snow beyond the area he had cleared.

He fired up the engine, the plane began to gather speed, then as it reached the end of the hardened snow, the motor went silent. He had tried to take off on an empty fuel tank. He never did that again.

Barr dug his snowshoes out and tramped out a new runway, then switched to the full tank, started the plane, and flew gracefully away while the temporary skis dropped off.

He took some ribbing from his friends in Atlin about staying so long at the lodge, where he was alone with Mary Joyce and her handyman. At the time he was dating Mary Kate Sands of Atlin, daughter of Clarence and Signe Sands.

He had known the Sands family since his arrival in Atlin with the Drinking Expedition. In fact, Barr claimed he was introduced to Signe, a strong-willed immigrant from Sweden, at the point of a gun.

It happened on a night when the Drinking Expedition was living up to its name. Clarence Sands, the jovial owner of Atlin's clothing store, was with Barr and several others at a party in Walter Street's cabin. As the clock struck one a.m. Clarence invited the revelers over to his house for a snack.

"We wandered down the street singing at the tops of our voices, having a good time. Evidently Mrs. Sands had just gone to bed and heard us coming," Barr recalled.

"Clarence and I went through the front door and she appeared at the head of the stairs with a double-barreled shotgun and said, 'One more step and I'll shoot. Get out of here.' " They left.

Clarence, an Englishman with a good sense of humor, always remembered that night. In his will he instructed that his 16-gauge shotgun be given to Barr, by then his son-in-law, as a souvenir.

Shell Simmons's Lockheed Vega at Juneau in 1937. The Alaska Steamship Baranof *is docked in the background.*

CHAPTER 8

Flying the Submarine

BARR HAD a standing joke with his wife that they weren't really married because he had paid for the wedding license with a bad check. He had just gone to work for Shell Simmons in Juneau and was between paychecks in June of 1937, when he married Mary Kate Sands of Atlin. Of course he flew back to Juneau and beat the check to the bank, but he was never one to ruin a good story with needless detail.

Barr got to know Mary Kate when he first moved to Atlin. For more than a year he lived in a tiny rented cabin behind the Sands' house.

Mary's father, Clarence, was born in Reading, England, in 1882, and had fought in the Boer War in South Africa. He came to the Atlin gold camp in 1907. His uncle Ed operated a small hotel in the nearby town of Discovery. In 1916, Clarence married Signe Wickstrom, who'd worked for him after he took over his uncle's hotel. They operated a clothing store until he died in 1952.

Mary and two brothers, Leslie and Lyman, enjoyed life in the old gold camp. Mary, the oldest of the three, had just turned twenty when she married Barr on June 30, 1937.

A small, thin woman with long dark hair and an easy laugh, she used to brag in Atlin that she was from the big city because she had been born in Vancouver. Mary went to grade school in Atlin, but there was no high school there so she was sent to a Catholic school in Prince Rupert, B.C. There she learned among other things how to smoke cigarettes. She was always a small town girl at heart.

Mary Kate Sands, Barr's future wife, sitting atop the Pilgrim, at Atlin in 1936.

Taking off from a snow-covered bar on the Tulsequah River.

Some years later when she and Frank lived in Fairbanks, they were driving their new Oldsmobile — the first one that came equipped with a turn signal — when she got upset with Frank for using it on a drive downtown.

"Don't do that!" she said. "People will think you're putting on airs!"

Mary learned to cook from her mother, and shared her father's sense of humor. People in Atlin told a story about when Clarence first went north: he wanted to ask for a job with a mining company that had thirty or forty men on the payroll. He caught up with the foreman on a tailing pile, but there were no jobs.

"What do you want me to do," the foreman asked, "Lay a man off and hire you?"

Clarence responded: "Oh no. For all the work I'm going to do, you don't need to lay a man off."

Mary's love of fun and skills as a homemaker complemented Barr's easy-going nature and big appetite. She also was much better at managing money than Barr and she kept the family afloat during many lean years.

They began married life with the security of a steady income, because Barr had started flying for Simmons about six weeks before the wedding. There wasn't enough traffic to justify his proposed Atlin-Juneau airline. Over the years Barr alternated between flying for himself and working for other men who knew how to run both an airplane and a business, such as Simmons.

The six-foot, two-hundred-pound Simmons first came to Alaska in 1925, as an electrician for the Alaska-Juneau mine. He and a friend who wanted to see more of the territory traveled the length of the Yukon River in a fourteen-foot boat.

Simmons worked in Nome for a time, learned how to fly in Yakima, Washington, near his hometown of Grandview, and eventually returned to Juneau.

"Shell was just like the rest of us. He was a laborer. He had no money, so he found a Santa Claus or two and he learned to fly. He bought a little Aeromarine Klemm," Barr said.

The Klemm's lack of power was demonstrated one day when Simmons and Barr tried to take off in it from Lake Washington in Seattle. Shell was tall and heavy; Barr was short and heavy.

"It was a calm day, no wind, and any way we tried it, it would not get off with the two of us. It was a two-place plane. It was overloaded with the two of us," Barr said.

On other occasions when Simmons had succeeded in getting the Klemm into the air and wanted to slow down, he'd simply stand up and let the wind resistance on his body do the trick. Simmons lost his first pilot's license that way, when it fell out of his pocket.

In 1934, a Juneau group acquired a Stinson for a new company called Panhandle Air Transport Company. Patco's Stinson, on Fairchild floats, was powered by a 265-horsepower Wright J6-7 Whirlwind engine, a powerful motor for a Stinson. The plane was nicknamed the *Patco.*

Simmons became the full-time pilot for the company in 1935, but the airline literally sank in Kimshan Cove when a storm sent the *Patco* under water for the first time. Before its flying days ended, the *Patco* had been submerged so many times that some took to calling it a submarine. Simmons bought the wrecked plane for $1 and began raising money in Juneau to rebuild it and start his own airline.

His company, Alaska Air Transport, grew into a solid, year-round airline. In 1968, the successor to his company became part of Alaska Airlines.

In the early years, as Archie Satterfield wrote in *The Alaska Airlines Story,* Simmons "went about building his airline with a vengeance, hauling anyone and anything anywhere.

"He delivered corpses. He flew a marshal into a potential shootout when some fish trap thieves were caught in the act. He delivered turkeys for Christmas dinner, dumping them out near the mine cookshack without landing. He delivered mail, and almost delivered babies when mothers-to-be waited too long for the trip to a hospital."

Simmons hired Barr to fly *Patco's* blue-and-gold Stinson, which by 1937 was near the end of its troubled flying career. The color scheme had a purpose: In case of a crash, the gold would show up in the timber and the blue could be seen against the snow.

When Barr started flying the *Patco,* its engine had been recently overhauled but the exhaust valves hadn't been replaced. Within a few months the bad valves caused five forced landings.

Lloyd Jarman, who worked as a mechanic for many years with various firms in Southeastern Alaska, recalls that Barr wasn't easily upset despite the limitations of the aircraft.

"Once he was loaded with passengers in the *Patco* and taxiing out for a takeoff, when the rudder jammed and swung him right into our hangar," Jarman said.

"When he pulled up and told me his trouble, I told him that was what he deserved for flying a pile of junk. The passengers heard me but Barr didn't care. Nothing bothered him."

Barr spent some long days flying the four-place Stinson that

In 1937 Shell Simmons hired Barr to fly his blue-and-gold Stinson, which Simmons called the submarine because it spent as much time under the water as on the surface.

summer, making half a dozen or more flights a day. The *Daily Alaska Empire* reported his comings and goings for one fourteen-hour work day under the headline "Pilot Barr and *Patco* kept in air full time."

The day before his wedding, Barr flew the *Patco* to Atlin, carrying the wedding cake as cargo. The prosperous Sands family had a big reception in their two-story house, which had been the hotel in Discovery and was moved to Atlin when the gold boom died.

Norm Fisher, a miner and local mailman, was the best man. The newlyweds left Atlin for Juneau with a big load of china and silver. They moved into an apartment in the center of Juneau.

On the trip back to Alaska's capital, Barr was in rare form as he cruised down the Taku River with ice-covered peaks rising to 7,000 feet on either side. The weather was good and he was feeling fine. He started singing at the top of his lungs, a practice he pursued in the air the way some men sing in the shower. His bride began to look at him in a funny way. Barr thought she was asking herself, "Who the hell did I marry? Maybe he is a little off."

After a busy summer working for Simmons, he and Mary took

Frank Barr and his wife, Mary Kate, in about 1940. (Courtesy of Winnie Acheson)

a vacation that fall, traveling south on the *Princess Nora,* the same ship that had brought him north five years earlier.

As the ship sailed through the calm Inside Passage waters, Barr struck up a conversation with Charles Whitney, a mining engineer and a man with a problem. Whitney's company had started gold mining the previous summer at a remote camp in the Fortymile Country, near the Canadian border in Interior Alaska. The North American Mines Company dredge on Jack Wade employed thirty men and Whitney needed someone to fly fuel and freight to the mining camp.

Barr thought the job would be perfect for his Pilgrim, but the engine needed an overhaul and he didn't have the money to pay for it. "Well, I'd never had such a thing as a contract before, where I knew I was going to eat. So I said, 'You just advance a little money to overhaul the engine, and I'll go in there and haul oil for you.' "

Whitney agreed and the two men shook on the deal. Barr was back in business, this time under the name Barr Air Transport.

CHAPTER 9

The Search for Barr

THE BIGGEST OBSTACLES he ever faced as a pilot, Frank Barr once said, were "boredom and hard work." He spent thousands of uneventful hours in the air, ferrying passengers and cargo over the roadless wilderness in complete safety. "But," he added, "now and then there was a little excitement."

One of the exciting times began at eight a.m. on August 4, 1938, when he loaded his blue-and-orange Pilgrim for what became the longest and most costly flight of his life.

The weather was clear and sunny and the 575-horsepower Hornet engine sounded perfect as he took off from Big Delta that day one hundred miles southeast of Fairbanks. He was carrying four barrels of diesel fuel for the North American Mines Company dredge at Jack Wade. The fuel was trucked up the Richardson Highway from Valdez to Big Delta and flown 135 miles to the mine.

Barr, who had moved to Fairbanks with his wife in the spring, had been flying from Big Delta to Jack Wade almost every day since April 3. It usually took an hour and twenty minutes to reach the mine.

After taking off that morning he climbed over a series of lakes and small mountains and was going about ninety miles an hour when the engine blew a cylinder. The plane quickly began to lose power and Barr couldn't hold his altitude. As he struggled to keep the plane going, he spotted a high, treeless ridge that looked like an excellent landing spot. He touched down as gently as he could

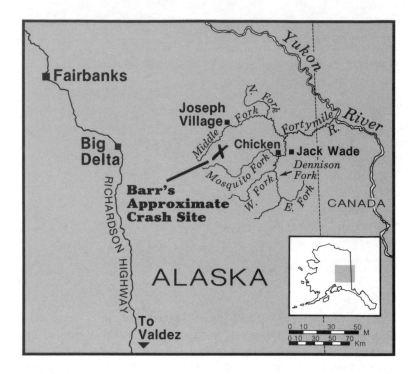

on the 4,000-foot ridge, but with nearly a ton of diesel oil aboard, the Pilgrim hit hard.

Beneath the inviting layer of thick moss he had seen from the air were jagged rocks that broke the tail wheel and shredded the rear of the fuselage. The plane quickly skidded to a stop and Barr, unhurt, got out to survey the damage. The tail section was in pieces and the plane's fabric was badly torn. An able mechanic by necessity and experience, Barr knew he'd have to get the plane back into the air because he couldn't afford another one. But at that moment, repairing the battered plane took a back seat to a more pressing concern — getting back to civilization.

Barr had no maps in the cockpit, but that made no difference. The only maps available were not very good, and he was going through familiar territory.

He was near the head of the Middle Fork of the Fortymile River, and about thirty miles southwest of the abandoned village of Joseph, where there were a few old cabins and a gravel bar big enough to land on.

Because he was down along a well-traveled air route between Big Delta and Chicken, Barr decided to stay with the plane. He couldn't call for help because he didn't have a two-way radio; a transmitter seemed like a high-priced luxury in 1938, for a small operator who was never sure where his next tank of gas was coming from. Barr did have a radio tucked away in his plane, but it was only a receiver for monitoring code transmissions, and it was broken. While he waited for help, he repaired the radio.

Like every pilot, Barr knew an occasional forced landing was the price of admission to the flying business and he had paid the price before. When trouble came, the bush pilot had to be a cook, hunter, trapper and woodsman rolled into one if he was to survive an unscheduled stop in the wilderness. There were twenty-two forced landings reported to the authorities in Alaska in 1937. Nearly all of the pilots survived. The planes flew slowly and the pilots had on-the-job training at picking out landing sites in an instant.

Barr had learned from his experiences in Southeastern and the Yukon, and he carried lots of emergency equipment. He had a couple of guns, rice and other dried food, matches, a gallon of airplane dope, tape, cooking utensils, fishing line and hooks, an ax, and mosquito netting in the Pilgrim. To help the search planes find him, Barr rolled out a barrel of oil behind the plane to supply fuel for a signal fire. He boiled some rice to take the edge off his appetite. Later he built a sod house, which was half dug into the ground, and sat there waiting to be found.

"There weren't many planes in those days and a missing one was quite an event. I knew they'd be looking for me."

It was late the next day when word reached Fairbanks that Barr was missing. There was no official organization to search for lost pilots, nor coordinate rescue efforts, so it was left up to volunteers. Fairbanks Mayor Les Nerland issued an appeal for funds asking citizens to donate money to look for Barr. Nerland said it was "urgently necessary" that "Pilot Barr and his plane be found as soon as possible."

"Lack of governmental provisions for such searches, which come periodically, is to be regretted and in time may be obviated," the *Fairbanks Daily News-Miner* said in an editorial backing the mayor's call. "But today an emergency exists that calls for spontaneous action."

One of the first pilots to volunteer was Frank Pollack. He flew over the route, but found no trace of Barr. Pollack said the area where Barr was believed to be lost was hazardous for a forced landing, but it would not be impossible to survive a crash in the maze of mountains, streams, lakes and tundra east of Big Delta.

The banner headline in the Fairbanks Daily News-Miner *on August 8, 1938, told of the search underway for Barr.* (Courtesy of the Fairbanks Daily News-Miner)

Soon Jim Dodson, Bill Lavery, John Lynn and pilots from Pacific Alaska Airways and Wien Alaska Airlines joined the hunt for the lost airman. So did K.S. Melsom, who rode in the Pollack Flying Service Bellanca with Lon Brennan. Melsom was trying something new in the search for a missing pilot in Alaska.

Using a Fairchild aerial camera, Melsom took 144 pictures covering 568 square miles of the wilderness where Barr was thought to have crashed. Brennan and Melsom spent three and a half hours at 17,000 feet without oxygen to take the aerial photographs, and they felt the effects after landing. Both had severe headaches and throbbing pulses for several hours after the flight.

The seven-by-nine inch films they brought back were quickly developed at the Co-Op Drug Store on Second Avenue in Fairbanks, and dried in a basement room of the Nordale Hotel down the street. There they began the search again, this time carefully examining negatives with magnifying glasses to see whether they could find any trace of Barr's plane. The pictures showed the country in great detail, but there was no sign of a Pilgrim.

Five days after Barr vanished, the *Daily News-Miner* headlined: "INTENSIVE HUNT MADE FOR AVIATOR BARR." But hope was dimming. Jerry Jones, a pilot for Pacific Alaska Airways, said: "We flew between 500 and 700 miles using binoculars and combing all the area in which Barr should have been. Barr is definitely down, and I think he's definitely in trouble."

As the search planes crisscrossed the country, Barr, who had learned the radio code in military training school, followed the progress of the PAA planes on his little receiver. But each time they just missed him.

"I listened and I heard the pilot in code saying, 'Going up Mosquito Fork. Nothing yet.' I ran out to light my signal fire," Barr said. "I had lots of diesel oil for a signal fire and by golly, he'd gone by. If he had turned around and looked back, he'd have seen my smoke. But he didn't."

By now Barr had seen six search planes come and go without spotting him, and he was running low on food and getting tired of what he called his "iron rations." To attract attention to his plane, he took pins and tape and put the word GRUB on one of the twenty-foot orange wings in huge letters and JOSEPH VILLAGE on top of the blue fuselage. Barr wasted no time when he heard another airplane coming. He quickly lit some diesel fuel and hoped the thick, dark smoke would be seen in the dusk. The winds kept the smoke close to the ground, but pilot Jim Dodson saw Barr's Pilgrim anyway.

"I flew low, circling the Barr plane four or five times, and waving to him," Dodson told a reporter. Barr waved back and pointed to the words "Grub" and "Joseph Village" on the plane.

Unable to land on the rocky ridge, Dodson flew back to Fairbanks, arriving at dusk shortly before ten p.m. At four a.m. a Wien Alaska Airlines plane left Fairbanks with supplies for Barr. It was piloted by Herman Lerdahl with Aeronautics Inspector Charles Burnett as a passenger.

They circled overhead, dropping food, a map, shoepacs, socks and a packboard for the stranded flier. Two hours later, they flew over and estimated he had covered about seven of the twenty-four miles to Joseph. Barr waved that he was all right and continued. The next two days proved to be a fairly easy hike for Barr, but the third day he spent mostly climbing and he went lame in one leg before he reached the gravel bar. He wasn't used to walking and he felt sore all over.

"When I got there my legs were so cramped, I just had to lie down on the bunk. I could hardly move," Barr said. He was picked up the next day by Pollack, who was returning to Fairbanks in his Bellanca.

Barr's Pilgrim on the Fortymile after he had rebuilt the tail and fuselage in the spring of 1939. "I always picked them up and brought them back," Barr said of the airplanes he wrecked during his quarter-century of bush flying in Alaska.

When the news that Barr was safe reached Juneau, the pilots who had known him said the story sounded just like Barr.

"Local and PAA pilots were not surprised today when informed that Barr has been found alive, for Barr has a faculty for getting out of messes." the Juneau newspaper reported. "Records show that Barr has had the public worried over his fate many times in the past, but today as usual, Barr is 'walking out, all in one piece.' "

Back in Fairbanks, Mary, who had told reporters all along that she expected Barr to survive, was elated when she heard that Dodson had found her husband, calmly tending a signal fire.

Barr returned home nine days after the forced landing. He was in good condition except for his sore legs and the loss of a few inches from his waistline.

Before 1938 was over he was to lose a few more inches, because he and Mary faced a long and difficult stretch with their meal ticket a crumpled heap on a lonely ridgetop. In later years Barr called it the "winter of the rabbit," he had shot so many to survive. Without his airplane he lost the Jack Wade contract to Wien.

They were living in a nine-by-twelve-foot shack he had built on a spot he rented near the air field in Fairbanks.

Mary Kate chopping wood. When the Barrs lived in Fairbanks in the early 1940s, their home was a nine-by-twelve foot shack located near Weeks Field. Their refrigerator was a hole beneath the floor, where perishables were stored in a bucket.

"It had two-inch planks on the bottom with a gap of about a half-inch where the fireweed used to grow up through. You know, we had pretty flowers on the floor," he said.

Their refrigerator was a hole beneath the floor, where perishables were stored in a bucket kept cool by the permafrost. Somehow they scraped by, and Barr mapped a battle plan to rescue his wrecked plane.

He learned how to weld that winter so he could rebuild the plane. When spring came, he took a small welding rig out to the ridgetop to attach a new tail section he had made in Fairbanks.

He spent two days digging the plane out of the snow, then slowly began to put it back together. After three weeks on the job, he was a "grisly sight to behold," according to a pilot who flew in a fresh supply of gasoline, but Barr worked on. He built another pair of disposable skis for the aircraft, like those he had used before on the Taku River.

The only way to test his first welding job was to fly the plane back home. He stamped out a runway in the snow, poured the oil in and started the engine. He had unloaded the diesel oil and left the welding tanks behind to reduce weight. The plane roared down the snow-packed runway and lifted off with no trouble. He flew to Jack Wade for gas, completing the trip he had started nine months earlier, and returned to Fairbanks.

"I have this thing about leaving an airplane," he said forty-three years later. "To me, an airplane has a personality, maybe a soul. When I flew an airplane for awhile, it was my friend. I wouldn't think of leaving one out in a swamp somewhere. I always picked them up and brought them back."

Back in Fairbanks, he asked Jim Hutchison, known to Fairbanks airmen as "Hutch," to reweld his repairs. Hutch, one of the finest welders in Alaska, inspected the plane and said it looked fine.

Decades later, Barr still thought Hutch's vote of confidence was one of the two or three real compliments he had ever received.

With his fledgling airplane business back in the air, Barr took out a tiny two-line newspaper ad to promote himself.

"For comfort and safety fly with Barr Air Transport," it said.

CHAPTER 10

Highways in the Skies

FAIRBANKS IN THE LATE 1930s was a log cabin town of about 3,000 with dirt roads and no running water outside the business district. But there were nearly four dozen airplanes based at Weeks Field and more flying than in the average town of 100,000. At the time it was the air crossroads of the North.

The town got its start when E.T. Barnette and his load of trading goods were unceremoniously dumped on the banks of the Chena River in 1901. For Barnette, it wasn't a matter of choice. The captain hauling him upstream refused to go any farther because of shallow water. Luckily for Barnette, an Italian prospector named Felix Pedro discovered gold the next year, sixteen miles away, touching off a gold rush that brought thousands to the newest boomtown.

By the late 1930s, Fairbanks had already gone around a few times on the economic roller coaster. The town nearly withered away during World War I, as the high-grade gold deposits were gone, but the construction of the Alaska Railroad and the arrival of the big gold dredges brought a postwar resurgence. During the 1930s, the mining camp of wooden buildings began to take on a more permanent appearance with the construction of concrete government office buildings, a movie theater and other improvements. The old wooden sidewalks were ripped up on Cushman Street and a $58,390 contract was let to make a five-block stretch the first paved street in northern Alaska.

Though a community celebration was planned to mark this latest advance in transportation, the real progress was in the skies overhead.

It began with Alaska's first flight, James Martin's ten-minute aerial show over Fairbanks on July 4, 1913. A decade later the commercial possibilities of the airplane began to be realized.

In the 1920s, Carl Ben Eielson, Noel Wien, Joe Crosson, Harold Gillam, Ed Young and others opened the door on the aviation age in Alaska. Just a few years behind them came Barr and a few dozen others eager to tap a growing reservoir of customers.

In the States, flying was still a novelty left largely to barnstormers and thrill-seekers. But in Alaska it quickly found paying clients among the miners, trappers and general public. Flying was faster and cheaper than traveling by dog team. It had taken forty days and $750 to reach Nome from Fairbanks by dog team. Within a few years, a Fairbanksan could fly the distance in five and a half hours, for $74.

"In a way," Fairbanks Mayor Les Nerland told the *Seattle Post-Intelligencer* in 1940, "Fairbanks is the most important aviation center in the world. Fairbanks people fly more miles per capita than any other people on earth. We are the hub of Alaska flying and we constitute one of the most important aviation crossroads of the Northern Hemisphere. The skies are our most practical highways."

Pacific Alaska Airways, the Alaska subsidiary of Pan American, was the largest carrier operating out of Fairbanks, flying Electras and Pilgrims. Alaska was an aviation laboratory in the eyes of Pan Am President Juan Trippe, who had learned from Lindbergh that the shortest and best route from the U.S. to the Orient was through Alaska. Objections by Russia and China delayed development of the Great Circle Route, but today 747s fly right over Interior Alaska on nonstop flights from New York to Tokyo.

In 1938, Trippe's airline had five miles of aviation routes for every mile of highway in the Territory, while a dozen other independent operators flew mail routes totalling 5,872 miles.

The smaller carriers did not have Pan Am's financial strength, so they had to rely on good service and low rates to attract customers from the competition.

Jim Dodson ran newspaper ads asking passengers to "Call Jim Dodson" if they needed aerial transportation. Dodson's personal delivery service got the supreme test in 1938, when a baby was born in his small plane on a flight from Ruby to Fairbanks. It happened a second time a decade later on a flight from Nenana. The night was cold and Dodson wrapped the crying newborn girl in his jacket on her inaugural flight.

In addition to local fliers, the Fairbanks airfield played host to

Fairbanks as it looked from the air in 1938, when the city was the air crossroads of the North. The local airport (Weeks Field) bordered the town on the south, and the winding Chena River is on the north.

aviators such as Wiley Post and Howard Hughes, who found it a convenient stop on round-the-world trips. As dignitaries spoke with the unshaven Hughes during his July, 1938, stopover, children scrambled near his Lockheed 14 to scoop up thousands of Ping-Pong balls dumped at the airfield to reduce the plane's weight.

The Ping-Pong balls, carried to help keep the plane afloat in case it had to be ditched, were not needed on the last overland leg of Hughes's flight to New York. When his plane departed with five and a half tons of gasoline aboard, it barely cleared the end of the runway, illustrating one of the continuing problems of Alaska aviation — lack of adequate facilities. Fairbanks was already starting to outgrow Weeks Field, which is home today to a small park strip and the Noel Wien Library, but the town didn't get a new modern airport until after World War II.

Radios were starting to come into use, but navigational aids were still nonexistent. The one government-supplied aid was a beacon atop the federal building downtown.

The lack of facilities was not the only sign of growing pains afflicting the flying business in Alaska. The number of passengers grew from 2,000 in 1929 to 32,000 in 1940, but there was never enough traffic to keep all the pilots in the black.

Aviators routinely undercut one another to get enough business to keep going, and a minority prospered. Rates for carrying the mail dropped, but only because of "extreme competition," a Civil Aeronautics Board investigator found.

"The financial condition of the industry in general was seriously threatened by a race for traffic, at rates which failed to take into consideration all the elements of the cost of maintaining an adequate transportation system," the CAB said later. "This resulted chiefly from the inauguration of services by 'one-man, one-plane' operators."

The owner/chief pilot/mechanic/cargo-handler of Barr Air Transport fitted that description exactly. With his plane back in the air by 1939, he went about arranging charter flights wherever he could. He flew one hundred barrels of oil between the Interior villages of Ruby and McGrath for a miner on Colorado Creek, and moved several tons of equipment for another miner at Chicken. He also helped fly in supplies for the construction of the airfield at Northway, one of several airports built just before the war for military and civilian aviation.

In the search for customers, all of the pilots were tough competitors, but Hans Mirow of Nome provided the classic example.

As Ray Peterson told the story, Mirow met the train in Fairbanks and picked up a load of passengers for Nome. He let them off in Tanana, however, telling them the weather was bad up ahead and he couldn't continue. He went back to Fairbanks and got more loads of Nome-bound riders, "caching" some in Ruby and some in Nulato. They all got to Nome eventually, in Mirow's plane instead of in Noel Wien's.

"It was a battle of wits," Peterson said of the flying competition. "It kept you alive and interested."

To cool off the competitive fever in Alaska, in 1939 the Civil Aeronautics Board moved to divide the Territory among the carriers. Under provisions of the 1938 Civil Aeronautics Act, the era of the free-roaming bush pilot was drawing to a close. The pattern of regulatory control which took shape then was not reversed for forty years.

After extensive hearings, the CAB granted certificates to nearly two dozen operators. Barr's was one of two applications rejected outright, and thirteen others were dismissed.

Barr had asked for the rights to fly from Fairbanks and Big Delta to the Fortymile District, to Barrow and intermediate points, to Harding Lake outside of Fairbanks, and to Whitehorse in the Yukon. The CAB explained its denial by saying Barr's occasional charter flights to those towns weren't enough to warrant awarding him a route.

The forced landing in the Fortymile Country was coming back to haunt him. The accident grounded him during the summer of 1938, the period in which Barr could have established "grandfather rights" under the regulations if he had been flying.

The CAB said: "The record of Barr's activities since he began flying on his own account thus reveals that he has not offered a continuous service to the public in any definite locality.

"We therefore find that the services proposed by the applicant are not required by the public convenience and necessity," the agency ruled on October 22, 1942.

Another Alaskan flier who was without an airplane during the grandfather rights period was Bob Reeve, who angrily denounced the regulations. Reeve's plane had burned in a hangar fire and the CAB denied his request for a certificate to fly the Valdez area, where he had operated for seven years.

"If we pilots who made Alaska what it is today had waited until the outlying bush and mountain 'required' airplane transportation by virtue of public convenience and necessity, this Territory would be today just about nothing but a worthless wilderness," Reeve wrote.

The sting of rejection didn't last long, however. Reeve went on to build a successful airline in the Aleutians, where the only competition he faced was from the weather.

In Barr's case, the CAB decision was also a blessing in disguise. He was soon hired by Harold Gillam for one of the toughest flying jobs in Alaska — the Kuskokwim mail run.

Heating the engine and oil in Barr's Pilgrim for takeoff. The steam-heated Pilgrim was comfortable for passengers in any weather, even though by the standards of the aviation industry it was an "old relic" by the 1940s.

CHAPTER 11

Airmail on the Kuskokwim

IT WAS FIVE below zero on the morning of February 21, 1924, when Carl Ben Eielson loaded 164 pounds of mail, a sleeping bag, ten days' worth of food, five gallons of oil, snowshoes, a gun and an ax into a De Havilland biplane at Weeks Field in Fairbanks. Bundled up in enough clothes to keep him warm at forty below zero in the open cockpit plane, Eielson started airmail service in Alaska that day with a two-hour, fifty-minute flight to McGrath on the Kuskokwim River.

Even though he got lost for more than an hour on the return trip, and broke a ski and the propeller when he landed in the dark at Fairbanks, Eielson's flight opened a trail that even the dog drivers could follow.

"I decided then and there that Alaska was no country for dogs," said Fred Milligan, who had hauled mail from Nenana to Flat and Bethel for twenty years by dog team.

Several years later Milligan went along with pilot Al Monsen as a guide on the first regular airmail flight to McGrath. Milligan loaded the plane and inadvertently delayed the trip by piling the entire thousand-pound load in the back, just as he would have done on his sled. After the pilot asked Milligan to move the sacks forward to even out the load, the plane took off and the guide watched in awe as the roadhouses and trail markers slipped beneath the plane's skis.

"It took him a day to do what took me twenty days," Milligan recalled in 1951, when he was Pan American's mail supervisor in

Harold "Thrill-em, Spill-em, No Kill-em," Gillam, the famed daredevil bush pilot, for whom Barr flew the Kuskokwim mail run in the 1940s. (University of Alaska Archives)

Seattle. "I could see the planes had the dog teams licked, so I decided to join with airmail delivery."

The last contract to carry the mail by dog team, on the run between Rampart and Fairbanks, expired in 1949. By then airmail was as much a part of life in Alaska as spring breakup.

Confidence in airmail service was built on the accomplishments of men like Harold Gillam, who had flown the mail on the Fairbanks-McGrath-Bethel route with the precision of a Swiss watch. Gillam had taken over the weekly 1,200-mile Kuskokwim mail run in 1938, and he prided himself on always getting through.

The people who lived in the dozen stops along the way claimed they could set their watches by the sound of Gillam's Pilgrim. In the early years the contract called for weekly flights between November and April.

Gillam was warming up his plane one day in McGrath when the engine caught fire and burned all the wiring and hoses. He sent word to Tom Appleton, his mechanic in Fairbanks, to get Barr to fly down with one of his two other Pilgrims. Gillam knew Barr well enough to know he needed work, and that he could handle a

Pilgrim. After Barr delivered the plane, Gillam continued the mail run and Barr waited for Appleton to repair the fire damage.

Appleton got the plane in operating condition, but he couldn't repair the gas gauge nor the airspeed indicator. On the flight back to Fairbanks, Barr began to notice their absence. A stiff headwind had slowed him down and the plane was running low on gas. As they crawled along with a ground speed of about forty miles an hour, both men knew the fuel situation was getting critical. Appleton was fidgeting in the back, looking down at the trees and worrying.

When the plane rolled to a stop on Weeks Field, there were only two gallons left in the reserve tank.

Barr made a few other flights for Gillam before he put him on the payroll full-time, in 1941. The two men never became close friends, but they got along well most of the time.

"He never told me how to fly or when to fly or anything else. I just flew the mail back and forth. I didn't know I had a boss, even," Barr said. "That's why I liked to work for him."

Like many pilots of the era, both had grown up in the rural Midwest and had run away from home as teenagers to join the service. Barr joined the Army at fifteen; Gillam was sixteen when he left Nebraska to join the Navy.

Gillam did some boxing in the Navy and learned deep-sea diving before he mustered out in 1923. He went to Seattle, where his parents were living at the time, took a ship to Alaska, and got a job operating a Cat for the Alaska Road Commission. Later he worked in Fairbanks, smoothing out the surface of the airfield. Spending most of the day at the airport, watching the planes come and go, sparked Gillam's interest. He decided to learn to fly.

During one of Gillam's lessons in a Swallow biplane, the aircraft spun into the ground, killing the instructor in Alaska's first fatal air crash. But Gillam's injuries were minor and he was back in the air before long.

Although he didn't even have a pilot's license at the time, Gillam became famous when he and Joe Crosson found the wreckage of Eielson's plane near the Siberian coast in January, 1930. The 32-year-old Eielson and mechanic Earl Borland had vanished the previous November, while hauling furs from an icebound schooner in the Bering Sea to Alaska.

What the *New York Times* called the "greatest rescue armada ever assembled in the Arctic" searched for the Eielson plane for more than two months that winter, fighting bitter cold and blowing snow. Crosson said it was like "flying inside a milk bottle."

Gillam's flying in those months earned him the respect of the flying fraternity. When his reputation grew, his penchant for flying in miserable weather led pilots to coin the term "Gillam weather."

"We used to refer to him as having a compass built into his head," Mudhole Smith once said of Gillam. "He always had a general sense of where he was."

A quiet man with heavy, dark eyebrows and a short, compact build, Gillam approached his job as if it was the most mundane task in the world. Although Gillam wasn't talkative, he was friendly even if he did have some peculiar habits. According to one account, he refused to have any lettering or numbers painted on his Pilgrims; he would hunt for anything except birds, and he didn't like having his picture taken. Outside his hangar he kept three caged polar bears that he had brought back to town as cubs from Alaska's North Coast. The bears had enormous appetites, and he gave them to a New York zoo when they reached two hundred pounds.

His wife once told an interviewer that Gillam's idea of a joke was to drop a biscuit on the floor while they had friends over to dinner. He would tap his foot on the floor just as it went down and say, "Oh, but they're good!"

When bush pilots were weathered in at some remote roadhouse, sitting around a wood stove, each with a drink in hand, they were prone to talk shop, recounting frightening or funny things that had happened in the air. Gillam, however, was not one for this kind of "hangar flying."

"At these times Harold would sit slightly in the background, grin at some of the more humorous remarks, and once in a while interject one of his own, but never offer information about his experiences," Barr said.

Barr went to work for Gillam Airlines after the Morrison-Knudsen Company, which had government construction contracts throughout the Territory, hired Gillam as chief pilot in 1941.

Once Gillam turned over the Kuskokwim mail to Barr, the people on the river could no longer set their watches by the mail plane, but Barr would have it no other way.

He flew through tough weather when he had to, often leaving Fairbanks under clear skies and hitting freezing rain near the coast, which would force him to land with ice covering the windshield. But Barr didn't feel compelled to take chances in bad weather. Bob Hanson, who flew with Barr as a mechanic on the Kuskokwim run, said, "If the weather didn't quite suit him, he just wouldn't go. If

The Kuskokwim
Mail Run

he didn't like the looks of it, he'd sit there for a day or two until it changed."

Barr said young pilots often get into trouble because they are afraid to turn around and go back.

"I never tried to fly like anybody else did. I knew what I could do and I knew my plane's limitations." Talking to pilot Oscar Winchell once after watching Gillam take off into a terrible snowstorm, Barr said, "He's got more guts than I'll ever have — you and me both."

When he had to fly in bad weather, Barr sometimes got help when he had no right to expect it. In the early days of World War II, radio silence was in effect at Alaska's airports because of fear that radio messages would help the Japanese. Barr was flying over McGrath one day and he couldn't see a thing through the thick cloud cover below him. He called in for the weather at McGrath because he didn't know what else to do.

"What's your ceiling there?" he asked the McGrath station. He got no reply. He was running low on fuel and he tried again, hoping the radio operator would bend the rules. Suddenly he heard a controller yell "Stinko!" over the radio. That adjective was

Postmaster Tim Twitchell of Akiak, a small village twenty miles northeast of Bethel on the Kuskokwim River, meeting the mail plane — flown by Frank Barr — in about 1943. Barr had landed on the frozen Kuskokwim River.

---

presumably not in the Japanese vocabulary, but it was enough to tell Barr what he was up against.

"I went back up the river a little ways toward Medfra, and I could see a little hilltop pointing up, and I knew how many bends there were down to the runway at McGrath."

He came down close to the river below the treetops and wound his way downstream until he reached the runway, which started just beyond a cutbank on the river.

"When I quit rolling I couldn't see either end of the runway," he said. "Of course, you do things like that when you're young and you've got lots of confidence and have an incentive, like not having enough gas to go anywhere else.

"Airliners today, of course, are not hampered one bit by lack of visibility, once they maintain their cruising altitude. But in bush flying in the older days, we didn't have all the instruments. We didn't have radio navigation aids."

Through good weather and bad, Barr flew the Kuskokwim mail run for the better part of four years, about a year longer than Gillam had flown it. The job was unlike any other in Alaska because it included twenty-four stops per trip, which probably gave Barr more landings per flight than any other pilot in Alaska.

On the 1,200-mile round-trip to Bethel he usually stopped at Lake Minchumina, Medfra, McGrath, Farewell, Stony River, Sleetmute, Crooked Creek, Napaimiut, Aniak, Kalskag, Akiak and Bethel.

The weekly journey through Southwest Alaska took four or five days during the winter. Barr would stay in roadhouses or with people he knew at different towns. His cargo could be anything from dried salmon for dog food to an entire dog team or rolled roofing. Barr's mechanic was Bob Hanson, later a vice president of Reeve Aleutian Airways in Anchorage. Hanson said that no matter what the load, Barr didn't take things too seriously.

"He always liked to joke with the people," Hanson said of Barr, "He had a good reputation." Hanson's job could be a dangerous one. For example, Barr remembered the time when he came in to land on an ice-covered strip and couldn't stop.

"I landed and it just didn't stop sliding. And old Bob, he could see that too. He jumped out on the ski and put his foot down and tried to stop it, and that didn't do any good either.

"I could see I was coming pretty close so I blasted it around on a sort of ground loop and slid sideways, then got clear around and gunned it in the other direction. Meanwhile, he was on this ski holding on for dear life. That's the kind of thing he had to go through."

Usually Hanson's chores were less harrowing. Every morning in winter he'd get up a couple of hours before daylight, to pick up the mail and warm up the plane. The engine oil was drained every night and taken inside the roadhouse, where it would be kept warm next to the wood stove. He'd get a plumber's firepot out of the Pilgrim's toilet, which wasn't used during the winter, and light it up beneath the engine, which was draped with canvas to conserve heat. After an hour or so, the warm oil would be poured into the motor and he'd start the engine.

Equally important on those cold mornings was an ice-free set of wings. The Pilgrim was a good plane for icing conditions, but Barr had learned early on, back in the Yukon, that a little ice can be big trouble. He once tried to take off with a little frost on the wings, expecting it to blow off.

"I gave it full throttle and I ran it two miles and it didn't even offer to lift off," Barr said. Light snow could be scraped off with a rope. Thicker ice required that the pilot climb up and carefully chip it away from at least the first third of the wing."

Barr enjoyed the Kuskokwim trips, because the weather was always a challenge and the people were always interesting. Except when he was stopping for the night or for a meal, he'd usually stay in the plane if he had his flight mechanic with him. He'd land wherever he could — which meant he rarely saw a real airfield.

"You'd have to go downstream to a bar like at good old Kalskag. They heard me coming on the radio and they'd go down there with a boat and meet me and give me the outgoing mail," he said.

Sometimes he left the mail in a barrel stuck on a sandbar which served as a village mailbox. In the summer he landed on gravel bars at most locations. In the winter he switched to skis and landed on the river ice. In times of flood, during spring breakup and just before freezeup, he saw his best landing spots disappear.

"The mail delivery was rather unorthodox. For instance, if I couldn't land at all, if the ice was moving in the rivers and the bars were flooded, I would circle over and Bob Hanson would kick the mail out in the swamps behind the buildings. I always wondered whether anything was breakable," he said.

One day he had a delivery to make at Sleetmute, a village just downstream from Stony River on the Kuskokwim. Ice in the river made landing impossible. The nearby Red Devil mercury mine had run out of carbide and needed more for its lamps. A small cannister of the chemical was in the mail that was tossed out of the airplane. It landed behind the village in the muskeg.

There were several Eskimos coming to get the mail, so Barr figured everything was under control. He circled around and headed downstream.

"Next day, a beautiful sunny day, I was kind of up high looking around the country and half asleep, and something ahead looked a little peculiar," he said.

As he approached the village, he noticed a huge dark cloud behind Sleetmute. But this was no ordinary cloud. He learned later it was smoke from a tundra fire which had started the previous day, after one of the villagers had carelessly discarded a cigarette near the package Barr had dropped. Luckily, the winds blew the fire away from the village.

On another occasion Barr learned that danger signals seen from the air aren't always what they appear to be. While heading toward Bethel with a ton of mail, Barr saw a native woman and two children run out onto the Kuskokwim River ice, waving frantically.

The woman made definite signs that the plane should land. Barr ran over the possibilities in his mind: perhaps her husband had been

Loading mail at Gillam's hangar in Fairbanks in 1942 for the Kuskokwim mail run. Frank Barr flew the Kuskokwim mail for about four years; on every 1,200-mile round-trip from Fairbanks to Bethel, he made 24 stops. For many bush villagers, he was their contact with the outside world.

injured. Or maybe he was away on his trapline and something had happened to one of the children. No matter what it was, Barr knew he had to land. He was the only contact these people had with the outside world.

A runway had been marked out on the ice with spruce boughs, but there were no ski tracks to indicate that a plane had landed there. Barr knew the snow was at least two feet deep and that it would be impossible to take off again with a full load.

He looked back at the cargo and couldn't even see Hanson, who was near the door in the only vacant space.

The plane slid to a stop in the deep snow and the woman breathlessly ran up to them with a broad smile on her face: "We're all out of tea — got no tea — you buy some you drop on way back — yes?"

It hurt too much to cry so Barr and Hanson had to laugh. There was no way the poor woman could understand all the work she had created for them.

"On the way back the next day," Barr wrote years later, "I got to thinking about what the charge should be — if I could collect. Unloading half a ton of freight near her house, flying downriver to a spot of glare ice caused by an overflow, unloading the other half, flying back to pick up the load left behind, flying downriver again and then reloading what we had left there."

As they flew over the cabin, Barr dropped the package of tea near the house and the mission was complete.

"I like to think of that Indian woman sitting in her snug cabin sipping her cup of hot tea, with no idea that she was drinking probably the most expensive cup of tea in the world."

---------- CHAPTER 12 ----------

Alaska Goes to War

THE OUTBREAK of World War II brought national attention to Alaska for the first time since the great northern gold rushes. This time there were no dreams of riches, however, only nightmares that Japan would attack America's northern frontier.

"I believe in the future, he who holds Alaska will hold the world, and I think it is the most important strategic place in the world," Gen. William "Billy" Mitchell told a Congressional hearing in 1935.

Two years later, Alaska Delegate Anthony Dimond said, "Alaska today could be taken almost overnight by a hostile force."

Their warnings were ignored.

Fairbanks was about fifteen hours' flying time from New York or Tokyo in the bombers of 1940. The airplane had played a crucial part in the development of Alaska in the 1930s and the Territory's residents flew more than any other people on earth, but it wasn't until war became imminent that Congress looked to the defense of the Territory.

In Fairbanks, construction began in 1940 on a $4 million cold weather test station which was to become Ladd Field. More than a thousand men worked on the base in three shifts. An endless procession of dump trucks rattled from the gravel pits to the new runway.

The new base was still under construction on December 7, 1941. With the Japanese attack on Pearl Harbor, Alaska went to war. The Army began mobilizing men and equipment in 1942 to build a highway connecting Alaska with the United States, and work at air bases across the Territory picked up speed.

Barr spent the war years on the Kuskokwim mail run, although he also helped form the Fairbanks squadron of the Civil Air Patrol, a group which practiced at Ladd Field, and he served as its commander for two years.

He was happier than ever to be getting a steady paycheck because his family was growing. As he and Mary K. put it in a birth announcement, the "first flight" of their daughter Sharon Alaska Barr was on December 19, 1943. The second child, Lynn Frances Barr, was born July 18, 1948. To accommodate his growing family, Barr built a new house which stood all alone at the end of the Weeks Field airstrip. He wanted to be close to the aviation scene, but sometimes it was too close. Big planes taking off from the field used to kick up stones that would hit Barr's picture window, which faced the strip. On one occasion a pilot forgot to reel in the radio antenna, strung out behind his aircraft. Just before he landed the lead ball at the end put a hole in Barr's roof.

During the war, the population increase brought on by the military buildup created a severe housing crunch. It became nearly impossible to find apartments in Anchorage, Fairbanks and Juneau. Rents ranged from $50 to $75 a month for desirable apartments, and some cab drivers could earn $500 a month. There was no rationing of food, except for local rationing of fresh milk. The larger towns voluntarily observed one meatless day other than Friday and prices for Seattle eggs ran about one dollar per dozen.

The Army undertook periodic blackouts during the war and their success was a matter of great pride to Col. Dale Gaffney, commander of Ladd Field.

"With very few exceptions they have been complete, and in each successive blackout marked improvement has been shown," Gaffney said.

Despite the restrictions and pressures of wartime operations, civilian aviation was showing big improvements as well, investigator Raymond Stough reported to the Civil Aeronautics Board.

He said pilots had started to fly trips on a set schedule, instead of letting takeoff times be dictated by the arrival of a full load.

"Advertisements appear regularly in Anchorage, Fairbanks and Juneau newspapers stating the days on which flights are made to named points," Stough reported to the CAB in July, 1943.

"The outstanding advertisement in this respect is that of (Art) Woodley in the *Daily Alaska Empire* of Juneau stating that his Lockheed Electra 'Arrives Juneau 2 p.m., Leaves Juneau 2:30 p.m. Tuesday-Friday.' "

Stough said there was a reduction in the number of ski and floatplanes operating in the Interior, as more operators were switching to wheels and using the airfields built throughout the Interior by the government before and during the war.

For some pilots, bookkeeping had once meant a wad of receipts stuffed in a shirt pocket. Now they had to hire accountants and keep formal records. Waiting rooms and new offices were built by many of the carriers, and the use of regular ticket forms became almost universal. Flying by credit was on a decline, Stough said. But some things hadn't changed among Alaska's fliers.

"There is still much trust in human nature, however," Stough added. "I saw, sitting openly and unguarded on a desk in the office of one carrier, a bag plainly marked as containing $7,980.99 in currency, being shipped by a bank to a company at an outlying point for payroll purposes."

Frank Barr's customers had great trust in him. The people in a dozen small villages along the Kuskokwim depended upon Barr for news, letters, groceries, packages, and general freight. Barr's nine-passenger Pilgrim also served as an aerial bus for short-haul passengers, and an ambulance during emergencies.

In early 1945, Henrietta McKaughan, a reporter for *Jessen's Weekly* in Fairbanks, accompanied Barr to get an idea of what a typical trip was like. After four days, twelve hundred miles and nearly two dozen stops, she concluded he ran a down-to-earth delivery service.

"Barr knows everyone on the river to Bethel, and his patrons know him so well they tell him what they want, rather than write orders to merchants," McKaughan wrote.

"If he gets mixed up at times and delivers Fairbanks eggs instead of Crooked Creek eggs to someone at McGrath — as he did — it's smoothed out somehow."

With three small kittens in a ventilated box and mechanic Bob Vanderpool as fellow passengers, McKaughan squeezed in with a mountain of cargo on her late-winter trip. Lake Minchumina was the first stop, a small settlement just north of the Alaska Range in the shadow of Mount McKinley. Vanderpool unloaded the mail and exchanged greetings with those who met the plane.

In a few minutes the Pilgrim was back in the air, heading southwest over the upper reaches of the Kuskokwim. The first major stop was 275 miles from Fairbanks at McGrath, an air crossroads on the Fairbanks-Bethel and Anchorage-Nome air routes. It wasn't unusual to find fifteen to twenty airplanes coming and going every

In Barr's one-man airline, the pilot had many duties, including sweeping the snow off the airplane.

day during good weather. When the weather turned sour, fliers from perhaps seven or eight different airlines would often find themselves killing time in the town, which ran a close second to Valdez as the "Poker Headquarters of Alaska," according to Bob Reeve.

"McGrath's airport is its 'Main Street' and planes are parked in front of business houses as automobiles are in a highway town," McKaughan wrote.

They went to the McGrath Roadhouse, an establishment in the center of town that always did a brisk business from the air trade. While planes taxied about, the travelers had a cup of coffee.

Before leaving McGrath, the mail sacks were readjusted to make room for mechanic Vanderpool's wife and niece. They had spent a week in McGrath, being attended to by traveling dentist Bart LeRue, and were going home to Crooked Creek.

The mail sacks for Stony River and Sleetmute were placed on top of the pile for an airdrop. Barr didn't plan on stopping at those two villages until the return trip, so Vanderpool would just kick out the sacks as they flew over. Barr changed his plans, however, when he learned by radio that there was a sick child at Sleetmute. They unloaded all the Pilgrim's cargo and passengers at Crooked Creek to make the plane as light as possible for the tricky landing on the river, flew back to Sleetmute, and picked up a two-year-old boy and his father. The child was running a high fever and had to be taken to the hospital at Bethel.

After the passengers and mail sacks were reloaded at Crooked Creek and Barr was back in the air, someone noticed the kittens had been left behind with Mrs. Vanderpool. Barr said he would pick them up the next week and deliver them to their new home in Aniak.

Barr landed on the ice at Napaimiut, and dropped his plan to fly all the way to Bethel that day because a storm had moved in. As the snow fell, they called it a night at Aniak, a little less than one hundred miles from Bethel.

In just about any weather, the passengers were comfortable in the steam-heated Pilgrim even though the plane was described by a national flying magazine, in 1944, as an "old relic" of Alaska aviation. The Pilgrim has proven to be as durable as the long distance traveler it was named for. N709Y, a Pilgrim Barr flew for Alaska Airlines in the 1940s and 1950s, was still being used to haul freight in Alaska until the early 1980s.

A crowd greeted Barr and his riders at Aniak, where it began to snow heavily. Barr made his way to the roadhouse where there was a big kitchen range like the kind used in most mining camps, a long table for diners, and a loft with bunks. The roadhouse was run by an old man who didn't care for customers who complained. One day a customer griped about the coffee being cold and the cook decided to solve that problem the next morning.

He took the customer's big, heavy mug and put it on the stove until it was red hot and the coffee was practically boiling. Before he rang the triangular bell for breakfast, he returned the mug to its normal resting place over the stove. The man came in, grabbed his mug, and cursed as he threw it to the floor.

"What's the matter," the cook asked, "Coffee cold again?"

After a night at Aniak, a good breakfast and not a word about the coffee, Barr was ready to take off. The skies were clear, but it was windy and the sick child whimpered in his father's arms on the rough flight. At Kalskag a dog team met the plane with a teacher and another patient for the hospital, a boy who had a bean stuck in his ear. After another short stop at Akiak, the plane arrived at Bethel.

A pair of Moravian church-workers had passed this way in 1884, on a day when the biblical text said: "God said unto Jacob, Arise, go up to Bethel, and dwell there, and make there an altar unto God that appeared unto thee." That's how the town of Bethel got its name and a Moravian mission. When Barr landed, a truck from the mission pulled up to haul the passengers and mail to town.

Barr decided to spend the night in Bethel. That way the hospital patients might be able to ride back with him, and the people in Bethel could answer mail immediately, instead of waiting until he came back the next week.

That night almost the whole town went to a baked bean dinner, movie and dance sponsored by the Bethel Women's Club. By Sunday morning, the weather had warmed considerably. The snow had turned to rain and parkas were shed for raincoats as the temperature hit fifty above.

Passengers who climbed into the Pilgrim for the return trip included a woman just out of the hospital, bound for Sleetmute, the child who had had the bean removed from his ear, and his teacher. The other sick child remained behind in the hospital.

As was often the case, the flight was a rough one. It was so windy that Barr decided it was unsafe to land at Kalskag. He landed on a slough outside of the village, knowing that the villagers would have heard and seen the plane and would send dog teams out to get the passengers and the mail.

After the Kalskag stop, the Pilgrim roared off into the north headed for Napaimiut, where Barr arrived at about the same time as a pickup truck driven by a fur-trader from Aniak.

The trader had driven over the Kuskokwim River ice with passengers on a fur-buying trip. The warm weather had melted most of the snow, and there was a layer of water above the ice.

Barr stayed overnight at Crooked Creek, in part because of the stiff winds and in part because Mrs. Vanderpool asked him to. She wanted her husband to spend a night a home. Because of the wind, Barr had to land quite a distance downstream from the village in a protected area, and men with dog teams came to take them to the village. They enjoyed a meal of reindeer meat and home-canned vegetables at the roadhouse.

Conditions were better the next morning and Barr stopped at Stony River and Sleetmute before landing at McGrath for lunch. After stopping again at Lake Minchumina, this time to pick up a trapper's wife, the plane arrived in Fairbanks as the lights of the city began to come on.

CHAPTER 13

Flying for Alaska Airlines

Harold GILLAM didn't think he was taking chances when he flew through bad weather, a friend once said, he was simply trying to achieve perfection in flight.

The goal eluded Gillam's grasp for the final time on January 5, 1943, when he crashed on a heavily timbered mountainside thirty miles east of Ketchikan. He was flying a ten-passenger Lockheed Electra from Seattle up the Inside Passage, when an engine failed during a violent storm. Gillam's plane broke out of the overcast at 2,500 feet, and he knew he couldn't climb over the mountains up ahead. He shut down the plane's other engine, pulled the aircraft up into a stall, and crash-landed in the trees.

One of the five passengers, a young woman, died 48 hours after the crash. The others were rescued 27 days later. Gillam wasn't so lucky. After the crash, he made his passengers as comfortable as possible and went off to set a signal fire and look for help. He was never seen alive again. Gillam's body was found on a beach seven miles from the crash site on February 3. The doctor who examined the body told Gillam's wife the flier probably died of a cerebral hemorrhage suffered in the crash.

Barr was one of the pallbearers at the funeral, in Fairbanks. Gillam was gone, but his airline lived on until after the war, when the remnants were sold. Barr made his last flight on the Kuskokwim mail run on September 16, 1945, a month after Japan had surrendered.

By then the defense buildup had done more to change Alaska and aviation than anyone could have imagined a few years earlier.

A 1,420-mile highway now connected the Territory with the United States. True, one travel writer complained that he rode by bus on the Alaska Highway from nine a.m. to eleven p.m. one day with only a cup of coffee for nourishment. But roadhouses soon appeared to take the edge off travelers' appetites.

More significantly, the government had spent more than $400 million to "build Alaska into a giant air base," historian Claus Naske has written. At war's end there were 56 radio ranges, 66 weather reporting stations and 24 auxiliary and intermediate airfields in Alaska. Instrument flight was now routine and Northwest Orient Airlines won the right to fly from Alaska to the Orient, using DC-4s at first.

There was still a need for bush pilots, however, and Barr got a job with Alaska Airlines, flying to small towns and mining camps.

Al Polet was the station manager at the time and Don Emmons and Johnny Lynn were among the other pilots. One of Barr's first assignments was to take a fast Bellanca Pacemaker on a trip to Slate Creek, near Wiseman. The landing strip there was built by the mining company on a steep grade. It was hard to tell exactly how steep the grade was from the air, however, and Barr had never been there before. As he tried to land going downhill, the runway kept dropping beneath his wheels. "I figured it would touch down any minute, but that just didn't happen. It just floated down there like a kite and the first thing I knew, when the wheels were on the ground, there was no more airport left."

He ran into the brush off the end of the runway and the plane nosed over, bending the prop.

"Al Polet was an easy-going sort of fellow and I guess he thought it was an accident," Barr said. "I guess it was in a way, but being stupid is no accident."

During his four years of flying the Kuskokwim, he had bent only one prop, and he would go on to fly for Alaska Airlines for a decade without bending another, but at that moment on Slate Creek he had his doubts about how long his career would last.

He had no doubts, however, about what he wanted to do. Bigger and faster planes were arriving on the scene, but Barr preferred small bush planes. He liked to navigate by watching the ground and he never warmed up to instrument flying. He never trusted what he couldn't see with his own eyes, and never earned an instrument rating.

Barr stowing emergency equipment into his plane during the days when he flew for Alaska Airlines.

Barr flew mostly bush routes for Alaska Airlines for nearly a decade. These mechanics are unloading a spare engine which Barr hauled to Slate Creek in 1947 for a downed plane.

"Modern airline pilots never see the ground," he said. "The bush pilots are watching the ground at all times. They're always looking for emergency landing places. They look at cabins out in the wilderness. They notice if there is any smoke coming up, if there's anybody around the place."

As usual, Barr's eyes were scanning the country beneath him the day he spotted a riverboat, full of equipment, drifted up on a sandbar in the Koyukuk River. He saw duffel bags, food and other supplies on the boat, but no people. He flew up the river about a mile, to a cabin owned by an eighty-year-old German fellow known as Old Dynamite.

Dynamite had suffered a stroke, but he still kept prospecting for gold every summer. It turned out he had been loading his boat when it got away from him and took off downstream. Barr landed and walked back along the riverbank, pulling the boat back upstream to Dynamite's cabin. Most other bush pilots would have done the same.

During his years with Alaska Airlines, Barr flew small planes on bush routes exclusively, and since the company took charters just about anywhere, he kept busy.

One winter day he had just come back from the Fortymile on a mail run, when a call came in that a man had died at Caribou Creek just twenty or twenty-five minutes north of Fairbanks. The old trapper had collapsed at his cabin, and the caretaker at the mine had hauled the frozen body by sled to the landing strip at Caribou Creek.

"I hopped in the little Cessna 170 and took the seat out in front alongside the pilot, so I'd have room to stretch the passenger out," Barr said.

The trapper had died with one arm stretched out above his head like the Statue of Liberty, and they couldn't bend the frozen body. So the mine caretaker, Barr and a third man carried the stiff, which Barr said was the right word in this case, out to the airplane.

The dead man's head was down alongside Barr's feet on the floor as he took off.

"I went along and scraped one side of the little valley to give myself room to turn to the left, and that darn creek kept climbing, and I kept climbing. Finally, I figured I could make it. I was nearly in a stall, though, when I turned and nearly scraped the other side of the valley. I felt quite relieved when I started down the valley instead of up," Barr said. "My passenger thought nothing of it though. He didn't say a word."

An aerial photo taken by Barr in 1938, looking down Taku Glacier to Taku Inlet. "Modern airline pilots never see the ground," Barr said. During his years in the air, he was always scanning the country for emergency landing places.

When he got back to town in late afternoon, Barr waved to mechanic Si Stadulis, who asked if he had any freight. Stadulis, who has worked for Alaska Airlines for more than forty years and is now the maintenance inspector on the company's Boeing 727s in Seattle, didn't know why Barr flew to the mine that day.

Barr said he didn't have much freight. "I've just got one piece if you'll unload it," he said. Barr walked into the shack near where the bush planes were parked, and waited. Soon the laconic Stadulis came in and said slowly, "This time I think you better unload your own freight."

Barr flew a variety of planes for Alaska Airlines — a Bellanca Skyrocket, a Norseman, a Gullwing Stinson SR-9 and a Pilgrim. He was based in Fairbanks most of the time, but he also flew out of Nome, Anchorage, Bethel, Bristol Bay and other points.

In these years, he dealt with many self-reliant trappers and prospectors who were accustomed to life far from town. Among them was an old-timer named Duval on the Fortymile River, who would put out a signal about twice a year for Barr to land.

"I'd see it going over on the mail run, and he'd give me an order to go into Eagle and bring out a full load of supplies from the store. I don't believe he ever went anywhere," Barr said.

One day in the winter Barr saw the signal, but this time it was not for a load of groceries. Duval was sick and wanted to go to the hospital in Fairbanks.

"He was in pretty bad shape. I helped him into the airplane and took him over to the hospital," Barr said.

The doctors diagnosed stomach cancer and they didn't give Duval long to live. He had a couple of relatives in Salem, Oregon, but he said he hadn't heard from them in years and didn't want to. Duval knew he was going to die and he told Barr to take the money he had on deposit with the Northern Commercial Company and give it to the Pioneers of Alaska. Then he gave Barr a gold watch, a timepiece the flier kept for the rest of his life.

Other bush customers made arrangements to be picked up many months in advance. Some of these were old trappers and prospectors who knew no other life. Others, like the pair of would-be miners he took to the south flank of the Brooks Range, were, as they put it, "tired of working for wages and weary of a job and city life."

All pilots took these flight arrangements seriously. Early in his career, Barr had promised to pick up two miners in northwestern Canada on a certain date. Even though he had injured his back and couldn't climb into the plane, he felt he had to make the trip. His mechanic hoisted him into the plane.

"I landed and the fellows were there. It was a lucky thing. I was all right as long as I didn't have to get in or out of the plane."

In the spring of 1948, Barr and Don Emmons had two similar experiences with old-timers who weren't particularly worried about watching the clock or the calendar. Emmons flew to Tibbs Creek to pick up William Eisenminger, whom he had dropped off the previous November. When the pilot landed, he found a note saying "Back in three weeks." As requested, Emmons came back later to return Eisenminger to civilization.

That same year, Barr had become alarmed when he landed at Dennis O'Keefe's cabin on the Koyukuk River and found no sign of life. No one in the sparsely inhabited area had seen O'Keefe at all that winter, and Barr could only guess at what had happened. Was he attacked by a bear and killed? Did he fall through the ice and drown? Did he freeze to death?

Barr got the answer two months later, when O'Keefe wandered into Wiseman hale and hearty. The tight-lipped sourdough would explain the delay by saying only that he "had some business to take care of."

There were never any guarantees about survival in the Alaska wilderness, however, and there were a few times in Barr's life when he wished he hadn't taken a passenger to the bush.

While working for Alaska Airlines in April 1946, Barr flew Charles Bernard Lapanski to the Sheenjek River country, about one hundred thirty miles north of Fort Yukon.

Barr had just come back from a long vacation to his old stomping grounds in Texas — and a long-awaited reunion with his mother and brothers. Lapanski told Barr that he had come from Shomokin, Pennsylvania, and worked in shipyards in Seattle and Portland. He came to Alaska because he wanted some excitement and decided to go prospecting. He had a lot of food, supplies and a dog when Barr dropped him off at the start of his gold-hunting expedition. The former shipyard worker said he didn't want to be picked up, and that when he was through he would build a canvas boat to float down the Sheenjek and Porcupine rivers to Fort Yukon.

When more than a year had passed and Lapanski had not returned to Fairbanks, Barr flew three hundred miles from Fairbanks to see what had happened to the prospector. His worst fears were confirmed. He found a tent, a cache, Lapanski's clothing, some bones and a diary.

In the diary, Lapanski told of the nearly seven months he had spent on the river. In his final entries he said that he wanted to kill himself, but he did not know why. The days on his calendar were carefully marked off until November 4, 1946. He wrote that he hated to do it, but that he would also have to shoot his dog.

Barr retrieved Lapanski's sleeping bag, wallet, diary and other belongings and handed them over to U.S. Marshall Stanley Nichols in Fairbanks.

Frank Barr signing the Alaska Constitution on February 6, 1956. He was one of 55 Alaskans chosen by the people of the Territory to write a state constitution.

CHAPTER 14

A Roving Bush Pilot

FRANK BARR had never taken an interest in politics until he filed for the Territorial Senate as a Democrat in 1948. He said there was no overriding issue that led him to run, just a feeling that he could do as well as some of the worst lawmakers and probably better.

"I just thought maybe I could improve things a bit."

He did little advertising in the campaign except for a newspaper ad that asked, "Who is Frank Barr?" in large type.

"Any old-time resident of the outlying districts can answer that question, but for the benefit of the newcomers to Alaska, he is now willing to let down his hair and tell all," the ad said.

"To the miner, trapper, prospector, trader in the isolated sections of Alaska, Frank Barr and his Pilgrim is a familiar and welcome sight." It went on to recount how he came to the North in 1932, and how he had spent all those years in the air.

"The moral to this whole story is: 'A rolling stone gathers no moss, but a roving bush pilot gathers a lot of information.' In running for Senate, Frank Barr believes he is better equipped than most to represent the people in the 4th Division because he has covered every part of it many, many times and is personally acquainted with so many of its residents."

His low-key approach to the campaign proved successful, particularly in rural areas, and Barr won easily. He ran for the Legislature three times and won twice, but he said his first year in Juneau was his best. "I was new. I didn't even know parliamentary procedure. But, by golly, I put in more bills than nearly anyone there," he said.

Legislator Barr was interested in civil defense issues and the Civil Air Patrol. In his eyes, among his chief accomplishments that first session were winning passage of a bill requiring pilots to carry emergency equipment, and the creation of a Territorial Department of Aviation.

Barr's bill on emergency provisions said every plane had to carry: enough food for every occupant to keep them alive at least two weeks, an ax, first-aid kit, one gun, a gill net and hooks and sinkers, a knife, two boxes of matches, mosquito headnets for every occupant, and two signaling devices such as colored smoke bombs.

During Barr's years in the Legislature, the lawmakers were basically divided into pro-Ernest Gruening and anti-Gruening factions. Barr was in the former.

"He was an intelligent man," Barr said of the Territorial governor and future U.S. senator. "He always succeeded in what he wanted to do, and that made people mad. Sometimes he was a little roughshod and rubbed people the wrong way, but he never did anything against Alaska."

At Gruening's urging, the 1949 Legislature enacted a comprehensive tax program for the Territory that was regarded as a major break from the domination wielded over the Legislature by the canned salmon industry.

Barr also got the chance to work closely with the Territory's other leading Democratic politician, E.L. "Bob" Bartlett, for many years Alaska's non-voting delegate to Congress. Bartlett also was later elected to the U.S. Senate.

In contrast to Gruening, Bartlett had a way of winning people over to his way of thinking. "I would say he was very effective because everybody was his friend. He didn't have to manipulate anybody," Barr said. Bartlett occasionally ate dinner at Barr's house near the end of the Weeks Field airstrip.

Barr got to see Bartlett in action when they flew together in Barr's Pilgrim on campaign trips. A group of five or six candidates would go from village to village for a week or two, meeting everybody, on the Alaska version of a whistle-stop campaign tour.

Bartlett, Barr and the other candidates would chip in to pay for gas and they would spend a day in each place, flying during the short days of fall and holding a community meeting at someone's cabin or a village meeting place at night. The weather on those campaign trips was usually bad, Barr remembered, and sometimes they had to stay two nights.

"Of course, we'd have a second meeting and try to think of

Barr served several years in the Territorial Senate. Here he is shown with the other members of the Legislature in 1957, seated in the middle row, nearest the camera. (Alaska Historical Library)

something different to say. This is difficult because the poor politician, he has what he wants to say and he says it in this village and the next village and the next village, until he gets damn tired of hearing himself say the same thing over and over again."

Bartlett, who dressed simply on the campaign trail, usually wearing an old plaid shirt like most Alaskans, handled these trips as well as anyone and was immensely popular among the Native people.

"Every village where we landed, they all greeted him like an old friend," Barr said. In 1952, when Bartlett was getting a strong challenge from "Glacier Pilot" Bob Reeve, Barr flew the delegate and a handful of legislative candidates to Akiak, Aniak, Sleetmute, Tanana, Alakanak, Barrow, Kivalina, Noatak and other towns.

At one point in that campaign, taking note of the popularity of John Butrovich and Mike Stepovich in the legislative races in the Interior of Alaska, Bartlett wrote Barr that in the next campaign they should file as "Barrovich and Bartlettovich" to be sure of getting re-elected.

Barr helped keep Bartlett informed of Reeve's campaign in 1952, and in one letter told Bartlett of a poster Reeve was using that showed the grim-looking pilot wearing an old flop hat pulled down over his forehead.

"You should have a lot of posters printed with his picture on it with the caption below 'This is Bob Reeve,' and then below that, 'Vote for Bob Bartlett.' "

Reeve's campaign slogan was "Get the Reds out of our government and our government out of the red."

When voters went to the polls that fall, Bartlett withstood the Republican challenge from Reeve, but Barr was trounced in the legislative race by Butrovich and Stepovich. He went back to flying until 1954, when he ran again and won.

Barr's relationship with Bartlett and his involvement in the Democratic party led him into one of the more notorious portions of his career — his brief stint as U.S. Marshal in Fairbanks.

The story began when, in Bartlett's words, "I sort of dredged his name out of nowhere" at a meeting in Fairbanks. Bartlett got the president to appoint Barr to the post and he took the job on April 30, 1951, with great hopes for his new career in law enforcement.

Almost immediately the new marshal came under pressure from two competing groups. One group wanted him to let gambling and prostitution continue in the bars and bawdy houses congregated in the south of town. The other group, led by the military, wanted the town closed down. They demanded that the marshal enforce the letter of the law.

Public opinion in Fairbanks had always been mixed about such vices. As far back as 1909, a federal investigator said, "The general feeling toward prostitution in Fairbanks is extremely friendly, to such an extent that the majority of the residents know the prostitutes by their first and second names."

Barr found himself caught in the middle. He and the city police enforced a ban on gambling in the city, but Barr also allowed the operation of a small "line" of about twelve to fifteen houses and three or four bars just outside the city limits.

"The marshal did not close this line because it was his belief that the class of people who patronized this district would be in the city causing greater trouble if a few such houses were not in business," the *Fairbanks Daily News-Miner* said at the time.

Meanwhile, Roy Webb, a Justice Department investigator, came to Alaska that summer to review the Territory's law enforcement problems. He found the marshals' offices in Juneau, Anchorage, Fairbanks and Nome greatly understaffed and said the high construction wages had attracted a lawless element that was entrenched just outside the city limits of the major towns.

"I found the areas surrounding Anchorage to be among the most wicked I have ever visited in all my life," Webb told his superiors.

"Crime is running wide open with very little check whatever. The jail in Anchorage is the biggest eyesore I ever witnessed."

When Webb arrived in Fairbanks on July 3, Barr came over to his hotel room for a visit. Webb asked what was happening with prostitution in Barr's district.

According to Webb's official account, Barr replied, "I heard that you were coming to town so I closed them up."

Those were not the crime-fighting words Webb wanted to hear. A few days later Barr resigned under pressure, feeling bitter about the whole affair. In his letter of resignation, he said there had been an organized campaign to discredit him by "the gambling element, aided by quite a few townspeople and merchants who want a wide-open town." Barr said they had succeeded in implanting "suspicion and distrust" in the minds of his superiors and had driven him from office after slightly more than two months on the job. Apparently, the people in the "gambling element" and those who wanted a wide open town told Webb that Barr was taking payoffs, which Barr said was a lie.

When he resigned, Barr went back to Alaska Airlines as manager of the northern division. All Barr said publicly at the time was that he had spent too many years in the flying business to feel comfortable wearing a marshal's badge.

He was more at home making laws than enforcing them. He won a seat in the Territorial Senate again in 1954, and the next year he was one of 55 Alaskans chosen by the people to write a state constitution.

The temperature was sixteen below zero when the Alaska Constitutional Convention began November 8, 1955, on the campus of the University of Alaska, on a hill four miles west of Fairbanks.

For much of the winter, the delegates worked long hours drafting a charter for the future state. Barr served on committees dealing with taxation and the structure of the executive branch. He spoke against setting the voting age at eighteen and gave himself as an example, recalling that he had joined the Army at the age of fifteen.

"That proves I did not have good judgment at that time and at nineteen I re-enlisted. That proves I did not have good judgment then."

He spoke forcefully for a bicameral legislature with its inherent checks and balances, and argued unsuccessfully that in addition to the governor, the commissioner of labor and other top officials should stand for election.

Barr also failed to get the delegates to drop the idea of calling local governments "boroughs." He said the word was foreign to Alaska and was used in England to separate cities.

"I am trying to get rid of the word 'borough' because I want to be able to walk down the streets without having people throw rocks at me," Barr told the convention.

Barr was one of only five delegates to oppose the article on local government. He said the article was well written, with the exception of that one word.

"Perhaps you think I am stubborn," Barr said. "I will agree with you."

On February 5, 1956, nearly a thousand people watched in the university's gym as the delegates ended their work. As each delegate's name was called to come forward and sign the document, the crowd applauded. Barr was the fourth delegate to dip his pen in India ink and sign the constitution.

The delegates produced a short, concise governmental plan for the State of Alaska still generally regarded as one of the best state constitutions ever written. The convention helped draw national attention to the Alaska statehood movement and bring about Alaska's admission to the union in 1959.

CHAPTER 15

Flying is Better than Working

TUCKED AWAY in the living room and bedroom of the old pilot's house were bits and pieces of a remarkable past: spurs from the Cavalry, an "inclineometer," one of the first airplane instruments used to determine level flight, hundreds of pictures of airplanes and aerial scenes taken in Alaska and British Columbia in the 1930s and 1940s.

He still had the mangled prop that had been trimmed with a hunting knife in the winter of 1933. There was also an old coffee grinder from Atlin, mukluks he used on the Kuskokwim mail run and a pair of snowshoes with his name on them that he had carried for hundreds of thousands of miles across the North. In his battered old flying logbooks he had carefully preserved the record of his flying career. Whenever he flew a different plane he'd write the model name on one of the back pages. The list grew to sixty planes and it included everything from a Jenny to a Supercub. He jotted down the time and date of every flight. When something unusual happened, he'd write a short note beside it. Terse notes such as these describe an age that has long since vanished.

"Plane turned over during storm. Repaired it and flew out six weeks later."

"Broken valve seat and cylinder head. Returned with dog team for parts."

"Forced down by snow."

"Landed account of weather. Snowed in three weeks."

"Forced down on mountain head of Middle Fork — engine failure."

"Search for Gren Collins."

"Search for Bob Hanson."

"Forced landing on Kuskokwim River. Broken push rod."

Elsewhere in Barr's house, mementos from Alaska's Constitutional Convention shared space with a ceramic figure of an Eskimo and dogsled filled with whiskey, which the pilot asked his old friends from Alaska to consume in a party after his death. He called his bedroom the Snakepit, because it was cluttered with boxes, papers and flying books.

Frank Barr, his sense of humor healthy to the end, lived out his last years in a one-story house on a tree-lined street in Grants Pass, Oregon, near the California border.

After he, Mary Kate and their two daughters left Alaska in 1956, Barr retired from commercial flying and bought a mobile home park in Portland. He was fifty-three when he called it quits as a bush pilot, twenty-four years after he had first sailed north to join the Drinking Expedition.

He couldn't stay away from flying, however, and after a few years he sold the mobile home park and went to work as a general aviation supervisor for a small company in Portland. Four years later he learned Spanish and conducted tours to Mexico and Alaska.

He and Mary Kate settled in Grants Pass in 1974, after he retired for a second time. She died in August, 1977, in her sleep.

After her death Barr energetically pursued his favorite hobbies of travel, photography and aviation. He loved to attend the conventions of the OX-5 Club, a group of pioneer airmen who cut their teeth on planes powered by the old OX-5 engine. The OX-5 was the first mass-produced power plant that gained wide acceptance among aircraft manufacturers.

The OX-5 pioneers gave him the "Mr. OX-5" award in 1979 as a "token of our admiration and respect for his laudable record of achievements in aviation activities."

He often drove his camper down to Mexico in the winter to "sit on a white sand beach under a coco palm and meditate, and watch the pelicans soaring over the surf looking for fish." His CB radio handle, displayed prominently by a sign on the back of his truck, was Polar Barr.

It would have been easier for him to take a commercial jet south every winter, but having spent so many years low to the ground, he liked to see the lay of the land as he traveled. He said modern-day planes are much safer and more reliable than those of his day, but "the fun is gone."

In 1976 a reunion was held on the campus of the University of Alaska, Fairbanks, for Barr and the other surviving members of the Alaska Constitutional Convention. Barr was then 73. He died from cancer seven years later.

"It's just like going into a hotel lobby and sitting down," he said.

Until his death from cancer in April, 1983, at 79, Barr kept getting his pilot's license renewed, and he borrowed a plane to fly every now and again. His license was reduced from a commercial to a private license when he was 76 because of bad eyesight, but he said that was to be expected.

"Let's face it," he said about that time, "I'm not an old bush pilot. I'm an antique bush pilot."

Once, without telling anyone he was a pilot, he attended a community college course in which the instructor told the students how important it was to determine mathematically how the weight should be distributed in a plane before takeoff.

"If I told them that I'd never in my life worked a weight and balance problem, and I'd carried millions of pounds of freight, they wouldn't have believed me," Barr said. "I can still remember that a case of milk weighed fifty-four pounds. And you loaded and balanced just right and you were seldom off."

Barr added, however, that he was thankful he had kept his mouth shut during the class, because the discussion among the young students showed him how much he didn't know about current flight practices.

"Nobody flies by the seat of the pants anymore. He does it using a slide rule, or now, an electronic computer," he said.

Though their methods were primitive by today's standards, Barr said that in looking back over his quarter-century of flying in Alaska, the pilots he knew had a record to be proud of.

"The bush pilot, generally, was of great importance to the country. Not only for transportation, but for delivering medicine, taking people to the hospital, weather reports, bringing fur-buyers around to buy the furs, practically everything."

In many places, all commerce except for heavy freighting depended upon the small band of men in flimsy single-engine planes. Not all pilots were cut from the same cloth, but Barr believed there were three basic types:

"There was the hell-for-leather, hard-drinking bunch. They just wanted to live life for what they could get out of it and have a good time.

"Then there was the larger middle class, which perhaps I belonged to. I'll let you judge that. They were fairly reliable. Maybe some worked hard, some didn't, but they loved to fly and they were in it for the flying.

"Of course, there was a third group, but very few of them, who liked to fly and had a business head on their shoulders and loved to make money."

Barr said Jim Dodson, the pilot who found him when he was lost on the Fortymile in 1938, was one of that rare breed. Barr also admired Dodson's way with words and said he summed up the life of the bush pilot quite well when he wrote:

"You've heard stories of old
About pilots so bold
  Who've faced the perils of storm
And carried the mail
In the teeth of the gale
  To rush the serum to Nome.
But over the bar when full of good cheer
  And Honesty's doing the talking,
They'll surely admit, except for the 'Drip'
  That Flying is better than working."

Sources

THE PERSONAL PAPERS of Frank Barr, which are still in the possession of the Barr family, including tapes, transcripts, logbooks, newspaper clippings and photographs, provided most of the information used in this biography. Several archival collections at the University of Alaska-Fairbanks were also helpful, such as the papers of E.L. "Bob" Bartlett and the papers of Ernest Gruening, and the records of the Alaska Constitutional Convention. The Truman Presidential Library in Independence, Missouri, was useful for information on Barr's short-lived career as the U.S. Marshal in Fairbanks. The following is a partial list of the periodicals and books consulted.

Periodicals

Alaska Life	*Fairbanks Daily News-Miner*
Alaska Sportsman	*Jessen's Weekly* (Fairbanks)
Alaska Weekly (Seattle)	*Juneau Daily Empire*
Anchorage Times	*New York Times*
Detroit News	*Popular Aviation*
FAA General Aviation News	*Seattle Times*

Books

Bilsland, W.W., and W.E. Ireland. *Atlin: 1898-1910: The Story of A Gold Boom*. Atlin: Atlin Centennial Committee, 1971.

Caidin, Martin. *The Silken Angels: A History of Parachuting*. Philadelphia: Lippincott, 1964.

Civil Aeronautics Board. *Report on 1943 Survey of Alaskan Air Transportaton.*

Civil Aeronautics Board. *Annual Reports of CAB, 1929-1943.*

Civil Aeronautics Board. *Alaska Air Transportation Investigation, 1942.*

Conot, Robert. *American Odyssey.* New York: Morrow, 1974.

Day, Beth F. *Glacier Pilot: The Story of Bob Reeve and the Flyers Who Pushed Back Alaska's Air Frontiers.* New York: Henry Holt, 1957.

Harkey, Ira B. *Pioneer Bush Pilot: The Story of Noel Wien.* Seattle: University of Washington Press, 1974.

Hinkle, Stacy C. *Wings Over the Border: The Army Air Service Armed Patrol of the United States-Mexico Border, 1919-1921.* El Paso: Texas Western Press, 1970.

Hinkle, Stacy C. *Wings and Saddles: The Air and Cavalry Punitive Expedition of 1919.* El Paso: Texas Western Press, 1967.

Hoagland, Edward. *Notes From the Century Before: A Journal From British Columbia.* New York: Random House, 1969.

Holland, Maurice. *Architects of Aviation.* Freeport, New York: Books for Library Press, 1971.

Hunt, William R. *Alaska: A Bicentennial History.* New York: Norton, 1976.

Jane, Frederick Thomas. *All the World's Aircraft, 1909-1940.* London: S. Low.

Janson, Lone E. *Mudhole Smith: Alaska Flier.* Anchorage: Alaska Northwest Publishing Co., 1981.

Jefford, Jack. *Winging It! His Own Story.* Chicago: Rand McNally, 1981.

Keith, Ronald A. *Bush Pilot With a Briefcase: The Happy-Go-Lucky Story of Grant McConachie.* Toronto: Doubleday, 1972.

Lutz, William. *The News of Detroit: How a Newspaper and a City Grew Together.* Boston: Little Brown, 1973.

Mills, Stephen, and James Phillips. *Sourdough Sky.* Seattle: Superior, 1969.

Naske, Claus-M. *An Interpretive History of Alaskan Statehood.* Anchorage: Alaska Northwest Publishing Co., 1973.

Naske, Claus-M. *Bob Bartlett of Alaska.* Fairbanks: University of Alaska Press, 1979.

Orth, Donald J. *Dictionary of Alaska Place Names.* Washington: U.S. Government Printing Office, 1967.

Oswalt, Wendell H. *Historic Settlements Along the Kuskokwim River.* Juneau: Alaska Division of Libraries and Museums, 1980.

Palmer, Henry Robinson. *This Was Air Travel.* Seattle: Superior, 1960.

Potter, Jean. *The Flying North.* New York: Macmillan, 1947.

Satterfield, Archie. *The Alaska Airlines Story.* Anchorage: Alaska Northwest Publishing Co., 1981.

Satterfield, Archie, and Lloyd Jarman. *Alaska Bush Pilots in the Float Country.* Seattle: Superior, 1968.

Smith, Dean. *By the Seat of My Pants.* Boston: Little, Brown, 1961.

Solberg, Carl. *Conquest of the Skies: A History of Commercial Aviation in America.* Boston: Little, Brown, 1979.

Taylor, Michael, and John Taylor, eds. *Encyclopedia of Aircraft.* New York: Putnam, 1978.

United Air Lines. *Airways of America, Guidebook No. 1.* New York, 1933.

Worthylake, Mary. *Up in the Air: An Aviator's Wife's Story of the Early Days of Commercial Aviation from 1924 to 1938.* M. Worthylake, 1979.

About the Author

DERMOT COLE has been writing about Alaska for nearly a quarter-century, as a newspaper columnist in Fairbanks and the author of four books. *Frank Barr: Bush Pilot in Alaska and the Yukon* was his first book, followed by *Hard Driving: The 1908 Auto Race from New York to Paris; Amazing Pipeline Stories: How Building the Trans-Alaska Pipeline Transformed Life in America's Last Frontier;* and *Fairbanks: A Gold Rush Town that Beat the Odds.*

Cole is a long-time newspaper columnist for the *Fairbanks Daily News-Miner,* writing about local history, personalities, politics, business, and doing personal essays.

He and his family live in Fairbanks.